7 Paths to Maximizing Your Social Security

What You Need to Know to Plan for Retirement

By Tony J. Hansmann

7 Paths to Maximizing Your Social Security: What You Need to Know to Plan for Retirement

Printed in the United States of America

First Printing, 2017

ISBN 978-1541148970

Cover Design & Interior Layout: Wesley Useche

Acknowledgment

There are so many people I want to thank. My dad who always found time. My mother who inspired me in many ways to be an entrepreneur.

To the many experiences with family, friends, and advisors and business partners. To my good friend and coach Matt Hausman who pushes me to think bigger.

To all my staff for putting up with my crazy ideas and lack of patience.

To my sister for all her business wisdom.

A very special thanks to my wife Gina, for encouraging me to live my dreams and giving me two perfect boys.

And finally to Jesus Christ for all His blessings and guidance.

Table of Contents

Introduction

Sometimes you receive a phone call that changes your life. For me it was several years ago — when someone I care about very much called me out of the blue.

Now I'll be the first to admit it. I was very busy when she called. So the first time she called I let the phone ring through. But a few moments later my phone rang again.

By the time I had picked up the phone all I could hear was her crying. She could barely catch her breath.

I didn't know what to expect — I was prepared for the worst: a car accident, cancer, a death in the family. A million things flashed through my mind. I felt sick to my stomach — then I heard it.

"Tony, I don't think I can retire, and I don't understand my Social Security options."

I've been working as a Financial Advisor for over 20 years and I have helped many people. Families, single men and women, rich and poor, young and old. But until that day I had never once put much thought into Social Security.

The reality is that most Financial Advisors don't want to deal with Social Security. In fact, they avoid it like the plague.

It's too complicated for them to figure out and it changes every time you bat an eye. They can't make any money off of it and generally they don't give you the time of day when you ask about it.

Later on that evening I told my friend I would find out everything she needed to know about Social Security and her retirement. I also made a drastic decision about my business.

I would provide everyone who stepped through my door with the most accurate Social Security information available. I would help everyone I talked to by giving them a proper plan on how to maximize their Social Security and give them confidence about their retirement.

The fact is, they need it. Social Security benefits have many different parts that are constantly changing. In fact, your benefits can be withdrawn in over 500 different ways.

I wrote this book to provide people with a simplified — but very complete overview of the entire Social Security system.

It covers the recent changes to Social Security. What the best strategy is whether you are single, married, divorced or widowed. How each benefit actually works and exactly how to avoid losing your benefits to excessive taxation.

I hope after reading this book you'll find that you have the information you've been looking for, you've calmed your fears about your retirement, and you're on your own personalized path to Social Security Maximization.

To Your Continued Success,
Tony J. Hansmann

Chapter 1
Social Security Overview

The first thing you need to do to maximize your Social Security benefits is to understand what the program is, how it works, and who it was intended to protect.

We take Social Security for granted now — it is a part of the landscape, and it feels like it's always been there as a safety net. However, that isn't the case.

In this chapter, I'll tell you a little bit about the history of Social Security to give you some context and a solid foundation to understand it. I'll also talk about what the Social Security Administration can and cannot do.

I believe this information is essential for anybody who wants to maximize their benefits. It's where I started when I wanted to help my friend, and it's where I want to start with you, too.

A Brief History of Social Security
The Social Security Act was signed into law in 1935 by President Franklin Delano Roosevelt, part of his New Deal. However, the roots of the SSA go back much longer than that.[1]

The idea of providing for people who need help is not a new one. In Europe, the establishment of so-called "friendly guilds" helped to protect tradesmen. These organizations were the precursors of two types of institutions we know well today: unions, and fraternal organizations such as the Elks.

By the 1600s, England had established Poor Laws[2] to help take care of the destitute, but these laws were rife with problems. For example, they made a distinction between the worthy and the unworthy poor.

All relief provided to the poor was locally organized. There was no government involved, so the amount given to the needy — and the people helped — could and did vary from location to location.

When the British colonized North America, they brought versions of the Poor Laws with them. They worked in a very similar way to the English Poor Laws. They were community-specific and often served with a side of judgment about the worthiness or unworthiness of potential recipients.

The first real mention of institutionalizing aid for the poor and elderly in the United States occurred in 1795. It came from famous pamphleteer John Paine.[3] He proposed a flat inheritance tax that would create a fund. His idea was that the fund would pay out a small stipend of 15 pounds sterling to every citizen upon reaching the age of 21 to give them a start in life and would then pay 10 pounds sterling every year after they reached the age of 50.

Over the years there were other variations of retirement plans. The U.S. Government paid pensions to veterans of the Civil War, as well as to widows and orphans of soldiers who died in the war. However, the government did not extend those benefits to Confederate veterans and their families.[4]

As industrialization spread, some companies began providing retirement benefits to their older workers, but those companies were in a distinct minority. By 1900, only five major companies were giving their employees some form of pension.[5]

At the same time, an Ohio politician named Jacob Coxey tried to organize unemployed workers to march on Washington to obtain unemployment benefits. He suggested using public works as a way of putting the unemployed to work — something Franklin Roosevelt would make a cornerstone of his New Deal.

By the 1920s, the United States had changed quite a bit. More people were living in cities than in rural areas, and for the first time, a majority of workers were dependent on paid wages to earn a living. That made them vulnerable to having their income affected by forces beyond their control. In that same time frame, medical advances increased life expectancies. It was clear that something had to be done to protect the elderly and ensure that they had enough money to survive after they retired.[6]

Several movements around that time aimed to put a system in place to provide for the elderly and retired, but none was successful. Here are three examples:

- Louisiana Governor Huey Long's Share Our Wealth program proposed creating a fund that would pay each family in the United States an annual salary of $5,000.[7]

- Dr. Francis E. Townsend of Long Beach, California, thought that the United States should instate a 2% national sales tax and use the proceeds to pay every citizen over the age of 60 a $200 monthly stipend. He called his plan the Townsend Old Age Revolving Pension Plan. His plan had over 2.2 million supporters by 1932.[8]

- Writer Upton Sinclair's End Poverty in California (EPIC) plan involved paying $50 per month to all California retirees who had lived in the state at least three years.[9]

There were many other such proposals in existence at that time, none of which caught on.

Then, in 1929, the stock market crashed, and the country entered he Great Depression. Unemployment skyrocketed, as did poverty. The crisis led to the election of Franklin D. Roosevelt as president in 1932 based on his promise to fix the problems that had led to the Depression.

When it was time to figure out how to provide for the United States' workers as they retired, FDR looked to Europe for answers. Instead of expanding welfare-based programs, he decided to create a social insurance program similar to those that worked in Europe.

President Roosevelt signed the Social Security Act into law in 1935. It put into place a national, contributory program that would allow workers to pay into a large central fund that would then pay out benefits upon their retirement.
In other words, Social Security is what is often described as a safety net, or an entitlement program. It combines worker contributions, which are done largely through payroll deductions, with a conscious social effort to provide for people as they retire.

When Roosevelt signed the Social Security Act into law in August of 1935, he acknowledged that the program was not — and could not be expected to be — a cure-all for poverty or the challenges of old age. He said:

We can never insure one hundred percent of the population against one hundred percent of the hazards and vicissitudes of life, but we have tried to frame a law that will give some measure of protection to the average citizen and to his family against the loss of a job and against poverty-ridden old age.[10]

The new Social Security board got to work. After a slight delay caused by a filibuster of the board's budget, they coordinated with the post office to mail out applications and issue Social Security numbers. By June of 1937, they had enrolled more than 30 million workers and opened 151 field offices.[11]

In subsequent years, numerous changes were made to the original law. One of the biggest changes was the extension of benefits to the spouses and dependents of workers, as well as the inclusion of a survivor's benefit to help support those left behind after a family breadwinner died.[12]

Monthly payments of Social Security benefits started with payments to a woman named Ida May Fuller of Ludlow, Vermont. She received her first check of $22.54 in January of 1940, and continued collecting monthly benefits until her death in 1975 at the age of 100.[13]

Today, the Social Security program is the cornerstone of many citizens' retirement plans. They receive regular mailings from the Social Security Administration advising them of what their monthly payout will be. For many people, particularly those who work in low-paying jobs or who have no savings, Social Security is the only retirement plan they have.

- As of December 2015, approximately 8.3 million people in the United States were receiving monthly Social Security benefits.
- Payroll taxes make up 86.4% of the Social Security Fund, with the remainder coming from interest (10.1%) and taxation of benefits (3.4%).
- The Social Security Fund took in more than $920 billion in 2015.[14]

One thing that has been proposed as a way of protecting Social Security is increasing the age at which workers are eligible for full benefits. The original retirement age was 65, but the current retirement age for people born between 1943 and 1954 is 66. That number increases to age 67 for workers born after 1960. An early retirement is an option at age 62, but the choice to retire early results in a permanent reduction to 80% of the maximum benefit.[15]

As you can see, Social Security is a massive program that benefits millions of retirees each year. For many workers who have lived paycheck to paycheck, it is the only retirement plan they have.

Navigating its benefits isn't easy. Even people who work with Social Security benefits all the time can be confused by them. Those who are getting ready to collect may end up feeling overwhelmed by the process, as my friend was.

Limitations of the Social Security Administration
Before I get into the specifics of how you can maximize your Social Security, I think it's important to touch on some of the limitations of the Social Security Administration. As I noted earlier, Franklin Roosevelt himself acknowledged that the SSA could not be a cure-all for poverty or the hardships of old age. However, many people who are preparing to collect benefits expect it to be.

Here's what the SSA can do:

- They can answer questions about filing for benefits.

- They can help you negotiate the death of a loved one and make sure their identity isn't stolen.
- They can help you navigate the process of claiming your benefits.
- They can help you deal with procedural issues that arise during the process.

It's important to notice what's **NOT** on that list because it's one of the primary reasons that people call the SSA.

*The SSA and its employees **CANNOT** give you or any other recipient advice about how to maximize your benefits.* [16]

I want to emphasize that point because it gets to the heart of why I wrote this book. The government employees who process Social Security claims, issue cards, and so on, are not qualified or authorized to answer specific questions about things like:

- Whether you should take early retirement
- When you should retire
- Whether you are better off filing as a survivor
- What you should do if you're divorced

Even if an employee of the SSA gave you such advice, there would be no guarantee that the information they gave you would be correct. Most of the people who work there are involved in the administrative end of things — processing claims, filing paperwork, and so on. It isn't their job to make sure you know all the ins and outs of maximizing your benefits.

It may be helpful to think of the SSA the way you think of the IRS. If you call the IRS to ask a question about your taxes, it doesn't absolve you of your duty to ensure that the amount you report is correct and that you take only proper deductions.

The same goes for Social Security. It isn't the Administration's job to help you maximize what you receive. It's their job to make sure that your claim is processed and that your monthly checks go out on time. They have some minor responsibilities when it comes to overpayments or underpayments, but they are largely an administrative organization.

Because it can be difficult to navigate Social Security laws as they apply to benefit amounts, taxes, and other issues, you need to take the time to educate yourself. It's the only way to make sure you don't end up settling for less than the full amount of benefits you are entitled to.

If you take the time to understand your benefits and evaluate them properly, then you will be certain to maximize your monthly benefits. You have options when it comes to how you learn about Social Security. You can hire a financial advisor with experience managing retirement and rely on them to help you make the best choices for your retirement. You can educate yourself and make sure you understand what your benefits are. Of course, you can also choose a hybrid of these two options — take the time to educate yourself, and yet also talk to an experienced financial advisor.

The key to maximizing your retirement benefits is understanding how Social Security operates, and how it can work with other retirement benefits that may be available to you. In the next chapter, I'll talk to you about the three-legged stool of retirement to help you do exactly that.

Social Security Advisors

The SSA and its employees CANNOT give you specific financial advice. An independent Financial Advisor with a Certified Designation is one of the best sources to obtain information on how to maximize your Social Security. Please visit with the Advisor who gave you this book or visit the following site for more information.

Visit www.SocialSecuritySupport.com

Chapter 2
Three-Legged Stool of Retirement

The ability to retire from working and enjoy the golden years of life without having to be part of the work force is an integral part of the American dream. Many of us dream of retiring early and doing the things that we don't have the time or money to do when we are young, such as traveling the world, pursuing cherished hobbies, or spending time with our families.

Before the passage of Social Security, such dreams were completely out of reach for anybody except the very wealthy and those who were fortunate (and frugal) enough to save enough money to allow them to retire. Today, we have, potentially, multiple options to help us prepare for retirement, including the following:

- Social Security
- Retirement savings
- Pensions

I like to call these the Three-Legged Stool of Retirement because they can work together to support retirees.
It is rare for any one of them to be sufficient, by itself
— especially since all three are in decline.

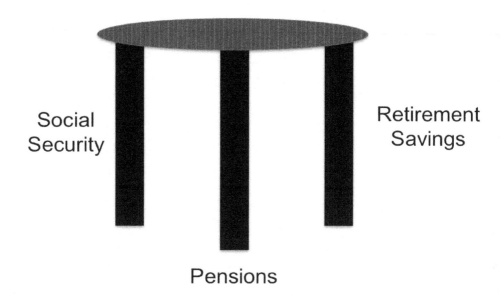

The possibility of retiring grows remote when any one of these three legs is weakened or removed. In this chapter, I'll talk about each one of these options and why and how they are threatened.

Social Security
In theory, Social Security should be self-supporting. American workers all pay into the Social Security fund when they work, and the money they pay determines the amount of their benefits.[16] However, there are some significant threats to Social Security and it's important for you to be aware of them as you move toward retirement.

- ■ Inflation can and does affect the cost of living as well as how far retirees can make their Social Security payouts stretch. The payouts do not always keep pace with inflation, and excessive inflation (as in the case of a prolonged recession or depression) could threaten the solvency of the fund.[17]

- In the past, there have been times when politicians have floated the idea of privatizing Social Security – making it a for-profit endeavor instead of a government entitlement program. [18] Such a move would certainly create problems for many of the people who rely on Social Security for their retirement.

- Social Security benefits were never intended to be a full retirement plan, but the percentage of income they replace is sometimes understated. Most workers receive only about 40% of their wages for an average of just over $1300 per month. [19] That's just barely above the poverty level and it points to a real weakness in the system.

While the threats to Social Security might not result in imminent collapse, they are real and should be taken seriously.

Retirement Savings
The second leg on the Three-Legged Stool of Retirement is made up of retirement savings — things like 401K plans, IRAs, and other investments. Such savings are optional, but many employers do offer matching funds as a way of incentivizing their employees to save for retirement.

As is the case with any investment, there is always a risk involved when you have a retirement savings plan:

- Economic stability is a must if you want a retirement plan to grow, and the U.S. economy tends to fluctuate on a regular basis. The economic downturn of 2008, which included the failure and near-failure of many large banks and financial institutions, took a big chunk out of many people's retirement savings.[20] Such crises are certainly not avoidable and anybody who relies on retirement savings as part of their plan for retirement has to be concerned about market fluctuations.

- While the intention might be not to withdraw money from a retirement savings plan until you are ready to retire, life has a way of changing things. Major events such as illness, the need to support an elderly parent, or excessive debt can force people to dip into their retirement savings early.

Those who manage to save a significant amount for retirement and who don't need to access their savings before they officially retire may be in fairly good shape. However, the arrival of a major financial crisis can have a drastic effect on even the most frugal and conservative investor.

Pensions
The third and final leg of the Three-Legged Stool of Retirement is the pension plan. Some people receive a pension as a reward for having worked at a particular company — or in a particular career — for 20 years or more.

Pensions are common for government employees. Traditionally, they have promised that in return for modest payroll deductions, workers could rely on a steady stream of passive income after their retirement.

However, like the other two legs of the retirement stool, pension plans are threatened. You can see how significantly they have declined on this graph, which compares pension plans to other retirement plans.

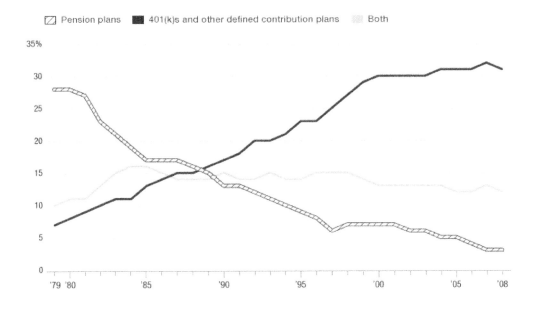

The downward trend is clear and troubling. Let's talk about why pension plans are threatened and on the decline:

- Most pensions were established with the assumption that they could sustain approximately 7% growth annually to keep up with inflation and be able to fulfill their obligations. That kind of growth was possible when interest rates were hovering around 5%, but in today's zero-interest world when government bonds are paying only about 2%, it's nearly impossible.

- Like retirement savings plans, pension plans rely on investments — and they are thus subject to the same market fluctuations and downturns as any other investment. If the stock market crashes or loses a significant portion of its value, pension plans suffer.

- Financial malfeasance has also contributed to the failure of pension plans. In the case of some large companies such as Enron, the financial mismanagement of the company and subsequent collapse of its stock gutted employees' 401k plans and their pension plans, leaving them hanging in the aftermath of the company's failure.

As you can see, the retirement stool might have three legs, but those legs are not as stable as we might wish them to be. Anybody who wants to be able to retire at a reasonable age should be concerned about the possibility of losing one of these three legs due to circumstances beyond their control.

What should be equally as obvious is that for many people, the collapse of any one of the legs on the Three-Legged Stool of Retirement poses a serious threat to their ability to retire. Someone who owns a home and still has a mortgage might not be able to afford to keep up with a mortgage payment if, say, they had to rely solely on Social Security. It's easy to imagine a scenario where that might be true.

Imagine a worker who retires and receives the average Social Security benefit of $1300 per month. This worker might have a spouse earning the same amount, but what if their mortgage is $1700 per month? They would be paying more than half of their combined Social Security benefits just to keep a roof over their heads.

The addition of money from a 401K plan, an IRA, or a pension might help — but it might not if their savings have been negatively impacted by inflation or stock market fluctuations. And if they withdraw too much from a retirement fund in any one year, they may be on the hook and have to pay taxes on a portion of the Social Security benefits — something we'll talk more about later.

You can see, I think, why you must do whatever you can to maximize your Social Security benefits. As I said before, the SSA is **NOT** able to answer questions or help you make strategic decisions about how to accomplish that goal. That's why I wrote this book.

Even if you have both retirement savings and a pension, you still need to look out for yourself by maximizing your benefits.

Guaranteed Income for Life

How strong is your Three-Legged-Stool?
How long will your money last?
For advice on how to guarantee you never outlive your money…

Visit www.SocialSecuritySupport.com

Chapter 3
Recent and Future Social Security Changes

One of the reasons that my friend was so scared and overwhelmed at the prospect of retiring is that Social Security laws and regulations are constantly changing. While the battle cry to privatize Social Security has quieted a bit in recent years, it has never fully faded. However, many of the people who campaigned for privatization have changed their tactics.

Instead, they have engaged in the steady erosion of benefits through small changes to Social Security. Think of it as the proverbial *Death by a Thousand Cuts.*

The reason for this slow erosion is that Social Security is a very popular program. Suggestions of cutting or eliminating it are usually met with a loud and passionate outcry, and it can be politically unpopular at best to say anything to threaten it.

The problem, of course, is that many Americans pay attention to legislators only when they are running. The rest of the time, they are not aware of what is being done to Social Security until and unless it threatens them.

As I have been writing this book, there have been some recent changes that took effect earlier this year that you need to know about.[21] In this chapter, I will outline those changes and walk you through what you need to know to navigate them.

The major changes that took place are as follows:

1. Full retirement age being pushed back for younger people
2. Elimination of dual benefits
3. Dependents cannot receive payments if you suspend your benefits
4. Lower raises to payouts each year (chained CPI)
5. Tax increases/changes
6. Increase to the maximum payout

Let's look at each one of these significant changes in turn.

Full Retirement Age Being Pushed Back for Younger People
The first thing you need to be aware of is a change — albeit a gradual one — in the age at which you will be fully eligible for Social Security benefits. When President Roosevelt established the fund, the age was 62. It has since increased and many of us still think of the age at which we can retire as 65. However, that is no longer the case.[22]

Here's how the retirement age breaks down:

- People born in 1954 or earlier can retire at age 66
- People born in 1955 can retire at the age of 66 years, 2 months
- People born in 1956 can retire at the age of 66 years, 4 months
- People born in 1957 can retire at the age of 66 years, 6 months
- People born in 1958 can retire at the age of 66 years, 8 months
- People born in 1959 can retire at the age of 66 years, 10 months
- People born in 1960 or later can retire at 67 years of age

As you can see, a gradual increase in the retirement age is happening. This is significant because the payouts you are eligible to receive can decrease significantly if you want to retire early.

Social Security Benefits by Retirement Age

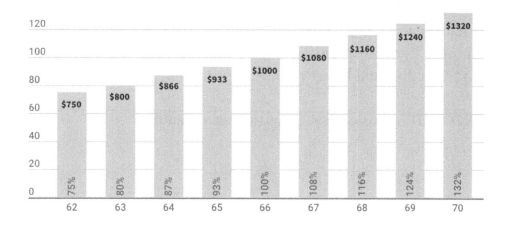

Later in the book, we will talk about the pros and cons of taking early retirement as opposed to waiting to reach full retirement age. There are benefits to both, and the key is understanding which option will work best for your personal circumstances. Retiring at the age of 62 might be the perfect decision for one person and highly problematic for another. Any strategizing you do will have to take your life and needs into consideration.

Elimination of Dual Benefits

Another age-related change that happened in 2016 has to do with spousal benefits — something we will cover in depth later in this book. For now, what you need to know is that it used to be that any worker could file to receive spousal benefits only, and then choose to receive their own benefits at a later date. The benefit of doing that was that they could allow their own benefits to fully mature. However, for anybody turning 62 on or after January 1, 2016, the option of separating the filings no longer exists.

To get a better idea of what this means in terms of benefits, let's break it down. Prior to this year, many spouses could receive up to 50% of their partner's benefits while deferring their own payments. That meant they could collect the spousal benefit up until the time they decided to switch over to the individual benefits based upon their own earnings.

As of 2017, that option is no longer available.[23]

People who plan to collect Social Security benefits may collect the higher of:

- A spousal benefit based upon their spouse's earnings; or
- An individual benefit based upon their personal earnings

There is no possibility of collecting both, a move which was expected to save the Social Security Administration approximately $10 billion over time.

Elimination of Suspended Benefit Payments for Dependents
Prior to 2016, it was possible for some people to find a way to allow their dependents — both spouses and children — to collect benefits by filing for them and then immediately suspending their own payments until a future date.

The reason for doing that was to allow their own benefits to reach maturity, increasing the monthly payouts they could expect to receive. For retirees, this move made a lot of sense. They could accrue delayed retirement benefits while still getting some money for their dependents.

As of May 2016, this option is no longer available.[24] Anybody who suspends their benefits after that date will cease receiving payments — and so will their dependents. Payments to dependents will resume only when you decide to end the suspension and start collecting your Social Security benefits on a monthly basis.

There is some benefit to suspending payments nevertheless. People who suspend and wait to collect until they are 70 stand to collect higher monthly payouts than those who begin collecting at the age of 66. The estimates are that people who elect this strategy end up costing the SSA approximately a half a billion dollars per year in increased benefits.

Later in the book, we'll go into more detail about suspending payments so you can determine whether doing so makes sense for you and your spouse or other dependents.

Lower Raises to Payouts Each Year (Chained CPI)
Another major change that occurred in 2016 and will continue to impact Social Security recipients for the foreseeable future is an alteration in the way annual increases are calculated. [25]

In the past, Social Security increases were tied to the cost of living — and that meant that the increases in payouts could vary greatly from year to year. Here's just a small sample to give you an idea of how dramatic the variations could be:

- In 1980, the increase was a reflection of massive inflation and totaled 14.3%
- By 1987, when the economy was in good shape, the increase was just about 4%
- In 2010, payouts stayed flat — there was no increase

This chart shows the fluctuation of payouts from 1975 through 2011.

Social Security Cost-of-Living Adjustments

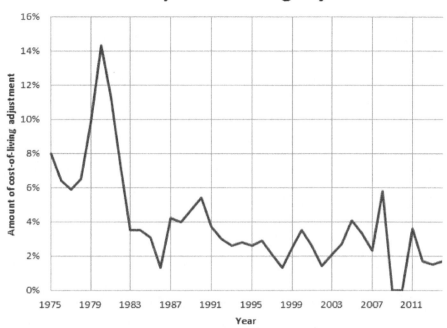

The increase for 2019 is only 2.8%, which will result in approximately thirty-nine dollars more per month for the average recipient, and about twenty dollars more per couple. That's a modest increase by any standard — and it has less to do with the cost of living than it does with a significant change in the way increases will be calculated going forward.

The Consumer Price Index (CPI) is a formula that tracks the way prices of consumer goods, including food, clothing, and other necessities change over time. It is used to determine cost of living increases for Social Security, food stamps, and veterans' benefits to name a few.

The change that happened in 2016 is that instead of using the CPI to determine annual increases in payouts, the SSA is now using something called a chained CPI. Simply put, the difference between the CPI and the chained CPI is that the chained version assumes that when prices increase, consumers will cut back by purchasing cheaper versions of the things they need. In other words, it passes the burden of saving money on to recipients — and makes no allowance for situations when cutting back might not be possible or practical.

The differences in real dollars are relatively small, and it might be tempting to dismiss them as insignificant. The average difference between the CPI and the chained CPI comes out to about 0.3%, which is only three dollars for every thousand dollars you receive. However, the differences become noticeable over time because they compound. Each year, the increase you receive is calculated based on what you already receive — so a 0.3% difference that reduces your benefits by $45 this year turns into more than $90 the following year — and so on.

For retirees who are trying to make every dollar stretch as far as it can, even minor adjustments in cost of living adjustments can make a huge difference to their comfort and quality of life. This change, in particular, underscores why it is important to learn about Social Security and do what you can to maximize your benefits.

Tax Increases
The third big change that you need to know about has to do with taxes. One of the keys to Social Security's solvency is the continuing payment of Social Security taxes by all eligible workers.

The current rate for Social Security taxes is 7.65% of income, which is matched by employers and paid into the Social Security fund.

Prior to this year, the cap on taxable income was $128,400 per person. In other words, if you earned a salary that was $128,400 or less, you would pay 7.65% in Social Security taxes on your entire salary. On the other hand, if you earned a salary of $129,000, you would pay Social Security taxes only on the first $128,400 you earned. Any income over that amount would be subject to regular income tax on both a federal and state level, but no Social Security taxes would be paid.

As of 2019, there is still a cap, but it's a higher one. The new maximum taxable income is $132,900. A person who made a $129,000 salary would go from having a small amount of income not subject to Social Security taxes to having their entire income subject to it. This change won't affect you if you are already retired, but it will if you are preparing for retirement.[26]

Tax Filing Status	Income	Taxation
Single or	Less than $25,000	0%
Head of Household	$25,000–$34,000	Up to 50%
	More than $34,000	Up to 85%
Married Filing	Less than $32,000	0%
Jointly	$32,000–$44,000	Up to 50%
	More than $44,000	Up to 85%

On a related note, there is also a change in the amount of money you can earn while collecting Social Security without experiencing a relative (albeit) temporary reduction in benefits.

- If you are 65 years old or younger in 2019, you can earn up to $17,640 without experiencing a reduction in benefits. For every two dollars earned over that amount, one dollar of benefits will be withheld.

- If you will turn 66 in 2019, the maximum you can earn increases to $46,920. For amounts higher than that, one dollar will be withheld for every three dollars you earn.

- If you turned 66 prior to 2019, no benefits will be withheld if you are still earning money, and your payments will be increased to include any money that may have been withheld earlier.

Increase in the Maximum Benefit
The fourth and final change you need to know about has to do with a small increase in the maximum benefit payable. [27] Just as there is a cap on the amount of income you must pay Social Security taxes on, there is a corresponding limitation to the amount of money you can collect from Social Security on an annual basis.

The increase from 2018 to 2019 is $73, bringing the new maximum to $2,861 per month. However, it is important to note that people who wait to retire until after the age of 66

— full retirement age — may be able to collect more if they defer payments.

These changes all have the potential to affect the strategy you use as you move toward retirement and make decisions about how to maximize your Social Security benefits. It is important to stay abreast of changes — and yet it can also be overwhelming. There are small changes to Social Security every year, and that's one of the reasons that my friend felt overwhelmed by the process of filing for benefits.

Now that you understand the basic framework of Social Security and how it works, and you are up-to-date on the changes that will happen in the coming year, it's time to dig into the process of maximizing your benefits. It's not enough to file and trust that you will receive what you deserve. You have to understand the process and make smart decisions — otherwise you risk leaving money on the table.

The next four chapters will walk you through what you need to know to move forward. I'll include tips to help you strategize for retirement, as well as information about individual, spousal, and survivor benefits. We'll also talk about the pros and cons of early retirement, how to plan for retirement, and how to reduce your Social Security taxes.

There Are Over 500+ Ways To Take Social Security

With all the ways to take Social Security…
And with all the changes to Social Security…
To get more advice, visit with the person who gave you this book or
…

Visit www.SocialSecuritySupport.com

Chapter 4
Social Security Strategy

When it comes to retirement, the key is not to enter into it blindly. Strategizing is important if you want to make sure that you are doing everything you can to maximize your benefits.

At first, navigating the many rules and regulations that govern Social Security can be tricky. There are literally thousands of rules to take into account and it can be overwhelming to figure out what to do and when to do it.

At this point, I would be remiss if I didn't note that it is simply not possible to cover every possible permutation of the rules in one book. The number of rules and the many possible variations in circumstances mean that there are countless possibilities. What is best for you might be very different from the solution that works for your co-workers or siblings.

The purpose of this chapter, then, is not to provide you with a definitive solution. Rather, it is to help you understand the basic foundation of Social Security strategy so you understand which rules and regulations are most likely to affect your payout.

I will walk you through the pros and cons of early retirement. While on the surface it might seem clear that waiting until full retirement age — or beyond — is the best choice, it might not be true for everybody. For some people, retiring early and accepting the reduced benefits that result might be exactly what is needed.

I will also talk about longevity and how it can affect your benefits over time. People today live much longer lives than they did when President Roosevelt first signed Social Security into law, and it is important to take that into consideration as you make decisions about how and when to retire.

Payouts are not the only thing affected by longevity. A related issue is paying for long-term care. As we get older and live longer, we also often require more intense care than we do when we are younger. There's no possible way to predict every outcome, but you should at least spend some time thinking about what you may need if you end up living for twenty or thirty years after you retire.

Finally, I'll close the chapter by giving you some guidelines to help you determine which options make the most sense for you. Again, it isn't possible or practical for me to provide detailed advice to everybody who reads this book. What I can do, instead, is to provide you with a list of questions and considerations to ask yourself so that you can make an informed decision about your future.

Should You Take Social Security Early?
I would like to start by addressing one of the most common questions I hear from my clients. While questions about social security can and do cover a wide range of topics, the thing I am asked most frequently is this:

When should I retire and start collecting Social Security?

There is a reason that I get that question more often than any other. The answer can vary from person to person, and the decision you make about this one key issue can have a huge impact on you now and for the rest of your life. It is not a decision to be undertaken lightly.

The decision is basically a calculated risk, no matter how you look at it. On the one hand, if you start collecting early you'll collect a higher number of monthly payments. On the other hand, if you delay, you'll collect fewer monthly payments over the course of your life, but they may be as much as 30% higher than they would be if you had retired at the age of 62. [28]

Before we get into the pros and cons of collecting Social Security benefits as soon as you are eligible at age 62, let's look at a graphic that shows the way early retirement can impact your payout depending upon when you retire.

Social Security Benefits by Retirement Age

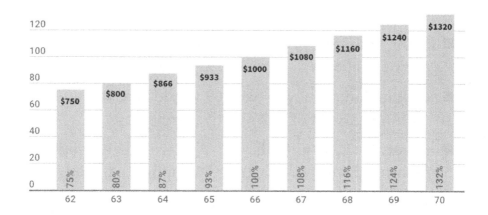

As you can see, the chart shows that there is a significant difference between the benefit that you might receive at the age of 62 and what you would receive if you waited until you were 70. Let's break it down:

- Waiting just one year and filing at the age of 63 results in an increase of $50 per month. That's a 6.7%increase.

- Waiting two years and filing at the age of 64 results in an increase of $116 per month, or a 15.5% increase.

- If you file at the age of 65, you would receive $933 per month, or a 24.4% increase.

- Filing at the age of 66 — full retirement age for anybody born before 1960 — results in a monthly payout of $1000, a 33.3% increase over what you would have received at 62.

- Waiting until the age of 67 to file translates to a monthly benefit of $1080. That's 44% more than the benefit you would have qualified for at 62.

- Filing at the age of 68 would result in a monthly payment of $1160, or a 54.67% increase.

- Holding out until you were 69 would give you a monthly payout of $1240, a 65.3% increase.

- Finally, waiting until the age of 70 would give you a monthly payout of $1320, or 76% more than you would have received if you had retired at the age of 62.

As you can see, those are significant differences. However, it would be a mistake to stop there. When you evaluate the best time to begin collecting Social Security, you also have to take longevity into consideration.

Let's say that somebody decided to retire at the age of 62. They receive $750 in monthly benefits. That would mean that by the time they were 70, they would have received eight years of benefits, or 96 monthly payments. What does that mean in terms of the overall amount you would collect?

ninety-six months times $750 comes out to $72,000 in benefits that our hypothetical retiree would have received before reaching the age of 70. That is a significant amount of money. You can see why it is important not to base your decision solely upon the amount of your monthly payout.

It would take approximately 126 months, or ten and a half years, for this retiree to make up for the $72,000 he missed out on by waiting to file.

Pros and Cons of Early Retirement

As you can see from the above example, there are some important considerations to keep in mind before making a decision about when to begin collecting Social Security benefits.

Let's look at the pros and cons of early retirement, beginning with the pros.

- The first and most obvious argument for beginning to collect Social Security benefits at the age of 62 is that you can collect a higher number of monthly payments – and potentially a higher amount of total benefits — then you would if you waited to start collecting.

- Another argument for collecting early is that if you have other retirement assets, such as a 401k plan, pension, or other investments, you may be able to invest the amount you receive from Social Security and parlay it into additional money that might make up for the fact that your monthly payments are not as high as they would be if you waited.

- If you have any health issues or other problems that might prevent you from working, then the benefits of collecting as soon as possible are clear. The money you collect — even at the lower rate that you would receive with early retirement — may be enough to support you and allow you to stop working.

■ Finally, there are some significant lifestyle and quality of life benefits to retiring early. For example, early retirement might allow you to do things like travel, pursue a new career or hobby, or spend more time with your family and friends. All of those things can translate into improved physical, mental, and emotional health.

What I hope you can see is that all of the arguments for taking Social Security early boil down to something that can be summed up with the old truism:

A bird in the hand is worth two in the bush.

In other words, there is a solid argument to be made that it is better to collect what you can now and do something with that money than it is to wait. Depending upon how long you live, you might be giving up thousands of dollars by waiting.

Now let's look at the cons of collecting Social Security early:

■ The first and most compelling argument against retiring early is that you will be getting a significantly smaller payment that you would if you waited and retired at the age of 70. If you have the desire and the ability to continue working, it may be worth it, particularly if you are in good health.

■ Another potential con has to do with your health. There is some evidence to suggest that people's health tends to decline after retirement unless they stay active. [29]

■ If you retire at the age of 62, you will have to find health insurance to tide you over until you are eligible for Medicare at the age of 65. Since health insurance is a considerable expense — and one that tends to get more expensive as we get older — that isn't an insignificant consideration, particularly when you keep in mind that the average monthly payment you receive from Social Security may be significantly lower than what you would receive if you waited.

The arguments against early retirement may be quite compelling depending upon your circumstances. You can see, I hope, why it is difficult to make any sort of blanket recommendation. A person who qualifies for early Medicare based on disability may be far better off retiring early than waiting, while someone who is still in good health and very active might choose to defer retirement and continue working.

Impact of Longevity on Payouts
One of the primary considerations to keep in mind when evaluating your retirement options is longevity. Obviously, it is not possible to be completely certain when you will die. People who are seemingly healthy can die suddenly as the result of an accident or an unforeseen illness, and people who are quite frail may prove to be surprisingly resilient.

However, there are some indicators that may help in determining the likely effects of longevity on your benefits — beginning with the United States government's estimate of average life spans for men and women: [30]

- The average man lives to be 84.3 years old
- The average woman lives to be 86.6 years old

If you recall our earlier example, we said that the person who waited until the age of 70 to begin collecting would need about ten and a half years to break even with the amount of benefits they would receive if they retired at the age of 62. In other words, they would have to live to be approximately 80.5 years old before the financial benefits of deferring retirement would kick in.

Looking at the average ages above, it is clear that the average person would end up collecting at least a little bit more, over time, if they waited until they were 70 to begin collecting Social Security. This graph illustrates the effects of longevity on Social Security benefits.

Impact of Longevity

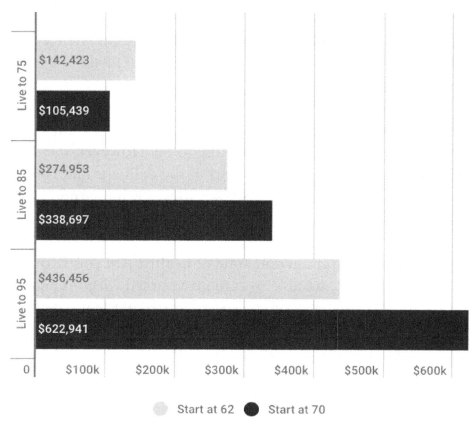

As you can see, a person who died at the age of 75 would be better off — to the tune of about $37,000 — if they started collecting early. However, the change reverses itself for people who live longer:

- A person who lived until the age of 85 would collect about $63,000 more if they waited until they turned 70 to begin collecting Social Security.
- A person who lived until the age of 95 would collect $186,485 more if they waited to begin collecting at the age of 70 than if they retired early and began collecting Social Security at the age of 62.

These differences are significant. When it comes to making a decision about when to start collecting, you will have to take your time and weigh all of your individual circumstances to determine which course of action is the most likely to benefit you in the long run.

Considering longevity — and by association, one's own mortality — can be a difficult thing to do. However, it is essential not to skip over this part of the deliberation. Here are some things that you may want to factor into your thoughts about longevity:

1. What is your current state of health? Are you strong physically and able to care for yourself without help?If so, do you have any reason to anticipate that situation will change in the foreseeable future?Obviously it is not possible to account for every possibility, but you may know — for example — that you have the early stages of arthritis or that certain diseases run in your family.

2. If you are married, what is the current state of your spouse's health? Here again, think about the present as well as anything you may know — or be able to guess —about the future.

3. How long did your parents and grandparents live?Life expectancy rates have increased over the years but often the lifespan of one or both of your parents can be an indicator of what your lifespan will be. If both of your parents lived into their nineties, then it is not an

unreasonable assumption to suppose that you might do the same.

4. Ask the same questions of your spouse if you are married. How long did their parents and grandparents live?

Once you have thought about these things, you can take a step back and think about how long you can reasonably expect to collect your Social Security benefits. If you anticipate a long life, then there is a strong argument to be made for deferring your benefits until you turn 70 if you can afford to do so. On the other hand, if you anticipate that you will need your benefits before the age of 70, it may be smarter to begin collecting as early as possible.

Determining the Best Option

To close out the chapter, I want discuss how you can decide which is the best Social Security strategy for you — and for your spouse and dependents. This is very much a numbers game, so I strongly recommend that you do some math to determine which option makes the most sense for your particular needs and circumstances.

You should begin by finding your most recent Social Security statement and reviewing it. It will include an estimate of your monthly payout at Full Retirement Age (FRA), and then estimates what your benefits would be if you waited until age 70 to retire or took early retirement at age 62. Here is a sample of what the statement looks like: [31]

Your Estimated Benefits

*Retirement	You have earned enough credits to qualify for benefits. At your current earnings rate, if you continue working until...	
	your full retirement age (67 years), your payment would be about	$ 1,680 a month
	age 70, your payment would be about	$ 2,094 a month
	age 62, your payment would be about	$ 1,159 a month
*Disability	You have earned enough credits to qualify for benefits. If you became disabled right now,	
	your payment would be about	$ 1,527 a month
*Family	If you get retirement or disability benefits, your spouse and children also may qualify for benefits.	
*Survivors	You have earned enough credits for your family to receive survivors benefits. If you die this year, certain members of your family may qualify for the following benefits.	
	Your child	$ 1,176 a month
	Your spouse who is caring for your child	$ 1,176 a month
	Your spouse, if benefits start at full retirement age	$ 1,569 a month
	Total family benefits cannot be more than	$ 2,908 a month
	Your spouse or minor child may be eligible for a special one-time death benefit of $255.	
Medicare	You have enough credits to qualify for Medicare at age 65. Even if you do not retire at age 65, be sure to contact Social Security three months before your 65th birthday to enroll in Medicare.	

* **Your estimated benefits are based on current law. Congress has made changes to the law in the past and can do so at any time. The law governing benefit amounts may change because, by 2033, the payroll taxes collected will be enough to pay only about 77 percent of scheduled benefits.**

We based your benefit estimates on these facts:

Your date of birth (please verify your name on page 1 and this date of birth)	April 5, 1974
Your estimated taxable earnings per year after 2014	$47,423
Your Social Security number (only the last four digits are shown to help prevent identity theft)	XXX-XX-1234

As you can see, this person would get:

- $1680 per month at their FRA of 67 years old
- $2094 per month at the age of 70
- $1159 per month at the age of 62

Beneath the statement of individual benefits there is also an estimate of disability benefits and survivor benefits. You may also notice that there is a statement about the probability of Social Security laws changing over time. It says:

Your estimated benefits are based on current law. Congress has made changes to the law in the past and can do so at any time. The law governing benefit amounts may change because, by 2033, the payroll taxes collected will be enough to pay only about 77 percent of scheduled benefits.

The last sentence illustrates why it is important to make careful considerations about when to begin receiving Social Security benefits. The amount listed is not carved in stone. It is calculated based on your highest years of income, but changes in the law and other forces — including overall economic strength — may affect the amount that you are eligible to receive.

In other words, the person in this example cannot assume that they will receive $1680 per month if they retire at the age of 67. They cannot even assume that 67 will be considered Full Retirement Age by the time they reach that age.

I know that sounds discouraging, but I feel it's important to be truthful about the realities facing retirees in this country. I would love to be able to tell you only reassuring things, and be confident that the amount your statement says you will receive is, in fact, what you will receive when you are ready to retire. It would be irresponsible of me to do so — so let's deal in realities.

As you prepare to make your decision about when to begin collecting the Social Security benefits you have earned, you must sit down and make some basic calculations. Here is what I recommend.

- First, calculate the total amount you would collect if you began to receive monthly payouts at the age of 62. You should do two separate calculations here:

- o The amount you would receive from age 62 until you reach full retirement age of 66 or 67 (depending upon your birth year)
- o The amount you would receive from age 62 until the age of 70

- Next, look at the amount you would expect to collect between the ages of 70 and 80 if you waited until the age of 70, and what you would collect in those years if you had started to collect at the age of 62. (Note: since it is impossible to predict cost of living increases, just stick with your estimated payout for these calculations).

- Figure out your break-even date — meaning, the point at which your total collected benefits if you waited until the age of 70 to begin collecting would outstrip your benefits if you began collecting at the age of 62.

For the person in our above sample, that calculation would look like this:

1. Monthly benefits based on early retirement: $1159
2. Monthly benefits based on retirement at age 70: $2094
3. Difference between monthly payments: $935
4. Total collected between the ages of 62 and 70: $111,264

To figure out your break-even point, all you need to do is take the total in benefits collected between the ages of 62 and 70 and divide it by the monthly difference in payments, like this:

$111,264 / $935 = 118.99 (This is the number of months it would take you to break even, so we'll round it up to 119)

119 / 12 = 9.916 (this is the number of years it would take you to break even, which works out to about 9 years and 11 months)

So, using this example, you would break even just before your 80th birthday.

Obviously, the numbers would be different if you wanted to figure out the difference between retiring at the age of 67 and the age of 62 because you would have to use a lower monthly payout to do the calculation. In that case, the calculation would be:

Difference in monthly benefits $521 ($1680 — $1159)

Total collected between the ages of 62 and 67: $69,540

Months to break even: $69,540 / $521 = 133.47, or 11 years and 1 month

Using this example, your break-even age would be 78, just about a month after your birthday.

After you calculate your break-even age based on your various options, take a minute to think about your expected longevity. If your health is poor or your parents died young, then it probably makes sense to start drawing benefits early
—

particularly if you have other means of income to support you such as a 401k or pension.

The important thing to keep in mind here is that it is just one potential tool to use when determining your retirement date. If you choose to wait to collect your benefits and end up dying relatively early, the possibility exists that you would die without having collected any of the Social Security you paid into over the course of your working life. On the other hand, if you begin collecting early and live a very long life, the decision to retire early might lead to you losing out on benefits that could have helped you in your golden years.

Other Considerations to Keep in Mind

What are some of the other things to consider before you make a decision about when to start collecting Social Security? Here are just a few:

- What other assets do you have, if any?
- Do you need Social Security in order to cover your current monthly expenses, or do you have other ways of paying the bills?
- If you're married, what are your spouse's benefits and when will they start collecting?

For example, if you have money from a 401k that you know you can draw on to meet monthly expenses, then you might decide to begin collecting Social Security early but invest what you collect. Alternatively, you might decide to wait until FRA to get a higher monthly payout.

On the other hand, if you do not have any retirement savings and will be relying 100% on Social Security to support you, then you'll have to decide if your benefits at the age of 62 will be enough to pay your monthly bills. If they're not and you can hold until FRA or even later, then you might be better off doing exactly that.

There is no hard and fast rule to help you decide when to begin collecting Social Security benefits. All you can do is look at your options, do some calculations, and then make the best choice based on what you know to be true. Certain things, such as how long you will live or whether you get sick, are impossible to predict.

I recognize that it might be frustrating not to have an easy answer to the question, *when should I begin collecting Social Security?* The best I can do is tell you that you should get as clear a picture as possible of your current and projected future financial situation and then go with the option that seems like it offers the potential for the least amount of financial stress over time.

The information in this chapter is largely based on individual benefits, but in the next chapter, I'll explain worker benefits, spousal benefits, and survivor benefits to help you understand additional variables that may factor in to your decision.

The Best Time to Take Social Security

Receive a Customized Social Security Maximization Report for you and your family. Have a Certified Social Security Advisor show you the best options by simply…

Visiting www.SocialSecuritySupport.com

Chapter 5
Social Security Benefits Overview

The amount of Social Security you can collect depends, as you know, on many different factors. The amount you earned while you worked and the age at which you decide to retire both play a role, but they are not the only things that figure into calculating your benefits. Your longevity also factors in, as does your marital status.

In this chapter, I will explain some of the ins and outs of calculating benefits, including information about worker's benefits, spousal benefits, and — in the event of your death or the death of your spouse — survivor's benefits.

Worker Benefits

Let's start with the one benefit that you can collect regardless of your marital status. The worker benefit is the benefit that you have earned over the course of your working life beginning with your first job. In your early years as an employee, you probably did not earn much.

Many of us start work in retail or food service. We work part time and earn a low hourly wage. Your benefits are determined in part by what your Full Retirement Age (FRA) is.

As a reminder, here are the FRA requirements and how they have changed over time.

Year of Birth	Full Retirement Age
1943–1954	66
1955	66 & 2 Months
1956	66 & 4 Months
1957	66 & 6 Months
1958	66 & 8 Months
1959	66 & 10 Months
1960 or Later	67

When it comes to calculating our benefits, the specific wages we earned – starting from our earliest jobs and ending at retirement — are taken into consideration. Over time, our wages most likely increase and in some cases, may increase dramatically. On the following page is an example of what I mean. [32]

Years You Worked	Your Taxed Social Security Earnings	Your Taxed Medicare Earnings
1990	654	654
1991	1.592	1.592
1992	2.854	2.854
1993	4.678	4.678
1994	6.367	6.367
1995	7.923	7.923
1996	9.985	9.985
1997	13.095	13.095
1998	16.232	16.232
1999	19.252	19.252
2000	22.240	22.240
2001	24.543	24.543
2002	26.341	26.341
2003	28.412	28.412
2004	30.970	30.970
2005	33.253	33.253
2006	35.799	35.799
2007	38.342	38.342
2008	40.065	40.065
2009	40.191	40.191

As you can see, this worker's annual income started off very low and then gradually increased every year.

The early years of work probably represent one or more part-time jobs. Those jobs eventually turned into full-time employment, and the worker in question received regular salary increases.

Eligibility for Social Security is on a credit system. People born after 1929 must accumulate 40 creditss in order to qualify to collect Social Security. As of 2019, one point equals $1360, so if you earned $5440 that year, you would have acquired 4 credits toward your Social Security eligibility. Most people can become fully eligible for Worker Benefits after working for 10 years.

You don't need to spend time calculating your Social Security benefits since the SSA does that for you, but I do think it's instructive to understand where the figures come from.[33] To do that, there are a few things that you need to know:

- Your Social Security benefit is based on your average earnings over the course of your working life. (For the purposes of the calculation, your working life means the 35 highest-earning years in your career.)
- Your earnings each year are adjusted for inflation — a necessary thing because many of us work 40 years before retiring and the pay we received early in our careers might seem paltry when compared to today's average incomes.
- The inflation used is calculated based on your base year, which is the year that you turn 60. So if you were born in 1950, your base year would be 2010. The average income in 1950 would be compared to the average income in 2010 to determine the proper inflation percentage to use.

The basic calculation, then, involves choosing the 35 years where you earned the most after the adjustment for inflation, and averaging the monthly payment from those years. The total earnings over 35 years are referred to as your Social Security dividend.

The other factor that goes into calculating your monthly benefit under Social Security is a sliding scale that is meant to help people at lower income levels in retirement. A person who earned close to the maximum income for most of their working career would end up earning a higher benefit in pure dollars than someone who earned a comparatively low amount. However, as a percentage of wages, the amount might seem low by comparison.

For example, a person who earned an average salary of $25,000 a year might get a replacement rate of 70% to help them in retirement, while someone who earned more than $100,000 per year might only get a replacement rate of 30% or so. This is where the "social" aspect of Social Security kicks in. It is meant to help people who might not have any other means of supporting themselves after retirement. Think of it as being similar to the sliding scale used for income taxes. As a rule, people in high income tax brackets pay a higher base tax rate than those who earn lower income.

Worker benefits are the simplest calculation to make because they are based only upon your personal work history and income and not on any other factors.

Everybody with a working history who has accumulated 40 credits is eligible to collect worker benefits.

The one thing you need to know here is that the worker benefits that appear on your Social Security statement may not represent the most you are able to collect. If your spouse earned more than you did, then you may be eligible to collect benefits from your spouse.

Spousal and Family Benefits
Keep in mind that Social Security is meant to provide a safety net for people after they reach retirement age. When the spouse or child of a retiree has been partially or totally dependent upon that person's wages for basic needs, it makes sense that they might also be eligible to collect benefits under the primary wage earner's Social Security.

Before discussing eligibility for spousal and family benefits it is important to note that having a spouse collect under your benefits does not reduce your payment. Their payments happen *in addition to* yours, not instead of them.

Here are the basic requirements to collect benefits other than your own.[34]

Current Spouse
If you are currently married to someone who is retired and collecting Social Security, you may be eligible to collect benefits based on their earnings.

To qualify for this benefit, your spouse (also called the worker) must be collecting benefits or have suspended benefits prior to May of 2016. You must be over the age of 62, unless you are caring for the worker's entitled child under the age of 16. The percentage of benefits you can collect breaks down as follows:

- If you are at full retirement age, you can collect 50% of the worker's full payment amount. You must have filed for Social Security yourself to qualify.

- If you are 62 but not yet at FRA, you can collect 35%of the worker's full payment amount. You must have filed for Social Security yourself to qualify.

- If you are any age but caring for the worker's entitled child under the age of 16, you can collect 50% of the Worker's full payment amount. This is the only option where you do not need to be retired yourself. However, the child must meet the benefits of entitlement — something we'll talk about later in the chapter.

It is important to make a point of discussing same-sex marriage since the laws have recently changed. The Supreme Court decision in *Obergefell v. Hodges* made same-sex marriage the law of the land. There was a brief period after that decision, which happened in the summer of 2015, when it was not clear how Social Security would apply to same-sex couples. However, the latest publication from the SSA makes it clear:[35]

We now recognize same-sex couples' marriage in all states, and some non-marital legal relationships (such as civil unions and domestic partnerships), for purposes of determining entitlement to Social Security benefits, Medicare entitlement, and eligibility and payment amount for Supplemental Security Income (SSI) payments.

Simply put, for the purposes of determining Social Security eligibility, same-sex spouses are now treated exactly the same as opposite-sex spouses. If you are married, then the guidelines above apply to you without exception. And if you are in a non-marital domestic relationship, you may still be eligible for some benefits based on your partner's income. It is a good rule of thumb to file even if you are in doubt about your eligibility.

It is important to note here that you may only collect under your spouse's benefits if the payment you would receive is greater than what you would receive if you collected worker benefits under your own name. In other words, if you earned more than your spouse, it makes better economic sense for you to file for personal benefits than to claim spousal benefits. As I mentioned earlier, there used to be a rule whereby you could claim spousal benefits if your spouse deferred their payments, and then claim your own worker benefits when you retired. As of May of 2016, that rule no longer applies.

Former Spouse
If you have ever gone through a divorce or you know somebody who has, you know that sometimes, there may be

an economic relationship — or even economic dependency — between two former spouses after their marriage ends.

The Social Security Administration acknowledges that fact, and makes it possible for divorced spouses to collect benefits under certain circumstances.[36] Here are the requirements to collect benefits as a divorced spouse:

1. You must be at least 62 years old, and there are **NO** exceptions to the age requirement. In other words, even if you are caring for your spouse's entitled child under the age of 16, you are not eligible until you reach the age of 62.

2. You must be unmarried. Just as is the case with alimony, the payment of spousal benefits does not extend to you if you get remarried. When you remarry, any spousal eligibility you have would be tied to your new spouse, not to your former spouse.

3. Your marriage to the worker in question must have lasted at least ten years for you to be eligible. The length of your marriage will be calculated from the date on your marriage certificate to the date that your divorce became final. If you decide to file for spousal benefits as an ex-spouse, you will likely have to provide both a marriage certificate and a divorce decree to demonstrate your eligibility.

As a rule, the Social Security Administration will check to determine if you are eligible for a higher payout under your former spouse's benefits than under your own, but it is best to know in advance if you can. You might not have access to your former spouse's Statement of Benefits, but if you know that they earned more than you during your marriage, make sure to keep that in mind when you are filing.

There is one more special rule regarding ex-spouses. Unlike current spouses, who must themselves have applied for Social Security in order to collect Spousal Benefits, you do not need to be retired yourself as long as you are over the age of 62. The reason for this provision is that as a former spouse, you have no say or control over the decision of when your former spouse retires – a decision that can have enormous impact on you if you require assistance.

In other words, if you decide that you want to file for Social Security at the age of 62 and your former spouse is 64 and still working, you can still collect benefits based on your relationship with them — even if they decide to continue working until the age of 70.

Dependents and Children

Now let's talk about dependents and children and when they can qualify or benefits. Here again, there are some specific rules that determine whether a child is qualified, or entitled, to collect payments under a parent's Social Security benefit. [37]

First, the child in question must be legally your child. A child may qualify if he meets one of the following requirements:

1. He is your legitimate child (meaning that he is biologically yours and was conceived within a marriage).

2. He is your natural child (meaning that he is biologically yours but was conceived outside of marriage) and you have acknowledged him as your child either in legal proceedings or in writing.

3. He is your legally adopted child.

4. He is your step-child (legally your child as a result of marriage).

It is important to note that these requirements apply to the children of same-sex couples the same way that they apply to children of opposite-sex couples. If you are married and you and your spouse have adopted a child, your genders and sexual identity play no role in determining the legal status of your child.

Assuming that the child in question is legally your child, there are other requirements that determine whether the child is entitled to receive benefits under your Social Security:

1. The child is under the age of 18.

2. The child is under the age of 19 and a full-time elementary or high-school student.

3. The child is 18 or older but under a total disability. To qualify, the disability must have started before your child reached the age of 22.

As a disabled child who qualifies for benefits, you may file at any time once you are over the age of 18. In other words, if your parent retires and begins collecting Social Security when you are 36 years old, you may file for Disabled Adult Child benefits immediately — and without having to adhere to the 5-month waiting period that normally applies to people who are applying for disability benefits.

The one thing to keep in mind here is that you will have to provide proof of your disability to qualify. A copy of your medical records is usually sufficient, but you should be prepared to demonstrate your entitlement to the benefits in question. As a disabled adult child, you are eligible to receive 50% of your parent's benefits. (Here again, the money you receive will not reduce the payouts received by your parent.)

Survivor Benefits
Earlier in this book, I told you that Social Security was intended to be a social insurance policy — something to protect people from poverty after they stopped working.

One element of Social Security that is put in place to protect the family members of workers, particularly those workers who are the primary breadwinners for their families, is the survivor benefit.

Simply put, survivor benefits are paid to your family, which may include your current spouse, former spouse, unmarried children, and dependent parents, in the event of your death. There are four basic types of survivor benefits: [38]

- Payments to your spouse if you were married at the time of your death, and/or to your former spouse if you were divorced

- Payments to children who survive you if they are unmarried

- Payments to your parents if they depended on you financially

- The above payments are all monthly, but the fourth option is a one-time, lump sum payment to your spouse or children

The thing that makes survivor benefits different from any of the other benefits we have discussed is that your family will be eligible to collect some level of payment even if you die well before full retirement age. For example, imagine a couple, John and Mary, who got married when they were both 21 years old. Twenty years later, John dies unexpectedly as the result of a car accident. He was the primary breadwinner for the family. In fact, Mary has spent very little time in the work force, choosing instead to stay home and raise the couple's two children.

Mary is only 41 years old when John dies, but she and her children — who are both under the age of 18 and not yet married — are eligible to receive benefits immediately. They do not have to wait until Mary is of retirement age. This benefit protects spouses of both genders, but it has been particularly helpful to women, who are more likely to stay home with children than men are.

Benefits Collected by Women by Source

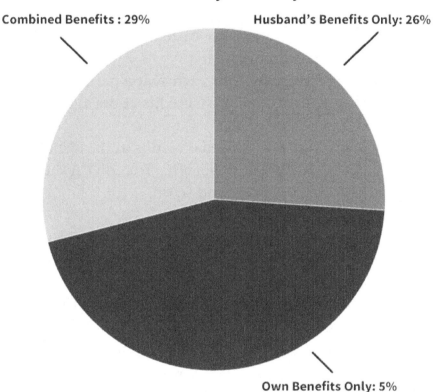

Combined Benefits : 29%   Husband's Benefits Only: 26%

Own Benefits Only: 5%

The determination of eligibility for survivor benefits still depends on a point system, but there is far more leniency in calculating it than there is for calculating benefits for a living person. While you must have accumulated a total of 40 credits to be eligible for Social Security upon your retirement, survivor benefits are calculated on a scale that makes allowances for people who have died before attaining full credits.

The chart that is used to determine the number of credits required is very simple. [39]
Here is how it works:

- People who die at the age of 28 or younger must have acquired a total of 6 credits
- Credits increase by 1 for each year a person lives, maxing out at a total of 40 credits at the age of 62.

In other words, you would need 6 credits at the age of 28 for your family to qualify for full benefits; 7 credits at the age of 29; 8 credits at the age of 30; and so on.

Looking at our example above, John — who was 41 years old at the time of his death — would have needed to earn 19 credits to qualify Mary and her children for fully insured status, meaning that they would be able to collect the maximum amount available to them based on John's average income. Remember, as of 2019, one credit was worth $1360. As long as John had worked for 19 quarters and earned at least $1360 in each of those quarters, Mary and her children can receive benefits.

Imagine, for a moment, that John had not met the revised eligibility requirements for Mary and her children to achieve fully insured status. Would that mean that Mary would be left without benefits?

The answer is no. Mary and her children under the age of 16 can still qualify for benefits as long as John had acquired 6 work credits in the previous 13 calendar quarters. (That means he would have had to do one and a half years of work in the previous three calendar years.)

In that situation, Mary's children under the age of 16 would qualify for benefits, and so would Mary as long as she was caring for children under the age of 16. However, Mary's benefits would end when she was no longer caring for any children under the age of 16, and she would not qualify for benefits as John's widow, because his work credits are not sufficient for that.

Now let's look at some of the specific requirements for survivor's benefits based on your relationship to the deceased person.

Widow/Widower or Ex-Spouse

If your spouse dies and you have been married for at least nine months at the time of your partner's death, you qualify as a widow(er) under Social Security and can collect benefits.[40]

Ex-spouses must meet the same requirements to receive survivor benefits as they would to receive regular benefits if their ex-spouse were still living. That is, they must have been married for at least 10 years, and they must be unmarried to collect benefits.

The rule about being unmarried applies to widows and widowers too, but in both cases, there is an exception. If you remarry after the age of 60, you may still collect benefits from your late spouse or ex-spouse. If you remarry before the age of 60, you may not collect those benefits.

The percentage of benefits you may collect depends upon your age and your marital status, as follows.

Widows and widowers may collect:[41]

- 100% of the worker's full benefit amount if they are at full retirement age or over
- 71.5% of the worker's full benefit amount if they are between the ages of 60 and full retirement age
- 75% of the worker's full benefit amount at any age if they are caring for the worker's dependent child under the age of 16

As stated above, the widow or widower must be either unmarried or remarried after the age of 60 to qualify for benefits.

Ex-spouses may collect: [41]

- 100% of the worker's full benefit amount if they are at full retirement age or over
- 71.5% of the worker's full benefit amount if they are between the ages of 60 and full retirement age
- 75% of the worker's full benefit at any age if they are caring for the worker's child under the age of 16

An ex-spouse must be unmarried or remarried after the age of 60 to qualify. However, an ex-spouse who is eligible because they have a child in their care will lose survivor benefits if they remarry. (In other words, someone who fails to qualify for survivor benefits on their own cannot receive any benefit — even if they are responsible for a worker's surviving dependent child — if they remarry at any age.)

It is important to note that there is a special category here for spouses of deceased partners who are disabled. They may claim a disabled widow(er) benefit if they are between the ages of 50 and 59. However, they must be classified as disabled within seven years of their spouse's death to qualify.

Here again, it is important to note that everything here about survivor's benefits for spouses applies equally to opposite-sex and same-sex couples. There was a brief period of turmoil at the SSA in the wake of the Supreme Court decision regarding marriage equality, but the SSA's position is now clearly stated on their website.

Another thing to be aware of is that survivor benefits are subject to change based upon early retirement. If you decide to take early retirement and begin collecting before FRA, your spouse's benefits will be lower than they would otherwise have been. They will be the higher of the following:

- 100% of the amount you were collecting; or
- 82.5% of the full payment amount

In other words, if a man retired at 62 and received a monthly payment of $1159, and his maximum payment if he had waited until FRA would have been $1680, his spouse would receive the greater of:

- $1159 (100% of the monthly benefit he was receiving); or
- $1386 (82.5% of the maximum monthly payment he could have received at FRA based on his income history)

This means that the widow of this man would receive a monthly payment of $1386. If he had not retired early, her payment would have been higher — she would have been eligible to receive $1680 per month once she reached retirement age.

Surviving Children

Your surviving children may collect benefits if they meet certain requirements. [42] In order to collect, a child must be:

- Under the age of 18
- Under the age of 19 and a full-time elementary or secondary school student
- Age 18 or over, but under a full disability that started before they were 22 years old

The maximum payout for each child is 75% of the worker's benefit, and is subject — as are the widow(er)'s benefits — to a family maximum.

There is also a provision for grandchildren of the deceased provided they meet one of the following requirements:

- The grandchild's parents must be either deceased or disabled; or
- The grandchild must be adopted by the surviving spouse of the deceased

In addition, the grandchild must have been financially dependent upon the deceased worker to qualify for benefits. In other words, your grandchildren cannot qualify for a survivor's benefit unless you financially supported them while you were alive. The survivor's benefit is meant to help people who relied upon you for financial support while you were alive. It does not extend to family members whom you did not support.

Surviving Dependent Parents
The final category of family members who may be able to claim a survivor's benefit after the death of a worker are dependent parents. If you care for your elderly parents and they meet certain requirements, then they may be able to collect a survivor's benefit – subject to the family maximum — after your death. [43]

To be eligible for a survivor's benefit, your parents must meet all of the following requirements:

- They must be your legal parent, meaning that they must either be your natural parent or have adopted you or become your stepparent before you reached the age of 16

- They must have been dependent upon you for at least 50% of their support before you died (or before your disability)
- They must be over the age of 62

If a parent meets all three of those requirements, they may collect one of the following:

- 82.5% of your full payment amount if only one parent is collecting; or
- 75% of your full payment amount (payable to each parent) if both parents are collecting

In either case, these payments may be reduced based upon the family maximum.

The strategies you apply when you file for Social Security may vary depending upon your eligibility and maximum payment and a number of other factors, including how many dependents you have and what your maximum family payment is.

In the next chapter, I will walk you through some strategies that can help you in each potential scenario, whether you have a current spouse, an ex-spouse, dependent children — or any other variation of family members who are eligible to receive benefits.

Popular Strategies

The most popular strategies are taught in this book. If you don't want to do it yourself there are certified advisors in your community that can do it for you! Visit with the person who gave you this book or

Visit www.SocialSecuritySupport.com

Chapter 6
Planning for Social Security

Now that you understand what your maximum benefit is and how the monthly payout you receive may vary based upon when you retire, your marital status, and other options, it's time to look at some strategies to help you plan for Social Security.

The strategy you choose will depend upon your marital status. The option that might be best for you if you were single might very well be detrimental if you are married or divorced.

Likewise, a person who has substantial retirement savings in the form of a 401k or pension plan might use a different strategy than someone who knows that they will have to rely entirely upon Social Security for income after they retire.

The goal of this chapter is to help you look at the big picture and make the decisions that are best for you and will allow you to get the highest possible payout.

I have broken the chapter down into three sections, with one each for strategies for single people, married couples, and people who are divorced or have been widowed.

Your individual circumstances may be such that you need to look at more than one of these options. For example, if you are married now but were previously widowed, you may still be eligible for payments under your late spouse's benefits if you remarried after the age of 60.

As you read this chapter, make notes of anything that may apply to you and your circumstances so you can refer to them later.

Strategies for Single People
To begin, we will look at the best Social Security strategies for single people. As a refresher, here are the specifics of eligibility for worker benefits. You must be at least 62 years of age to file a claim for your own benefits unless you are disabled. The age requirement specifies that you may file a claim the month after your 62nd birthday. In other words, if you turned 62 on October 15, you could file for Social Security benefits on November 1 of that same year.

The one exception to this rule applies to people whose birthdays are on the first day of the month. The reason is that technically they attain the age of 62 on the last day of the previous month. So, if your birthday fell on October 1 instead of on the 15, you would be eligible to file for early retirement benefits on your birthday instead of having to wait a month like other retirees.

The other consideration is that, as previously noted, you must have accumulated 40 work credits. If you reach the age of 62 and do not have enough credits, you have two options that would enable you to file for Social Security and collect benefits: [44]

1. You might qualify to receive a benefit under your current or former spouse's benefits; or
2. You could work enough to reach the requirement of 40 credits and then collect.

Remember, the worth of one credit as of 2016 is $1260, so if you earned only $5,040 that year you would earn all four credits for that year. However, the fourth credit cannot officially be earned until the first day of the last quarter of the year.

Imagine that you had 36 credits as of the end of 2015 and you wanted to work enough to be able to collect Social Security. You might earn $5,040 in the first quarter of 2016, but you would not be eligible for Social Security until October 1 of that year.

As previously discussed, the payment you would receive if you filed at the age of 62 would be significantly less than what you would receive if you waited until full retirement age (FRA). You will have to take that into account when making a decision about when to retire.

One number that you need to know about when you are strategizing for Social Security is your Primary Insurance Amount or PIA. [45] The PIA is the amount that you would collect if you retired at Full Retirement Age. It is calculated using three different "bend points" — markers that help the SSA calculate the amount of benefits you are qualified to receive.

This chart shows the PIA bend points for 2016 for individuals:

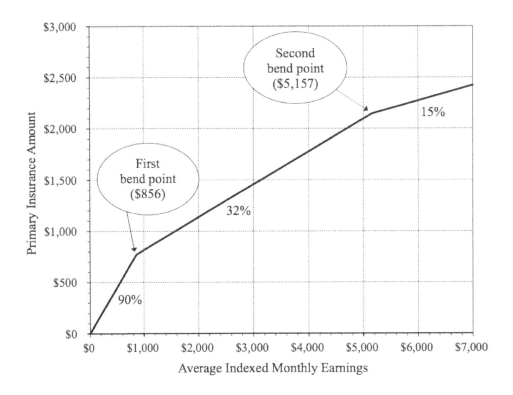

Basically, the calculation for your benefits works like this. You get:

- 90% of your income up to the first bend point, which on the chart is $856 of your average indexed monthly earnings
- 32% of your income between the first and second bend points, which on the chart would be between $857 and $5157

■ 15% of your income after the second bend point,
which on the chart would be amounts over $5157

To get an idea of how it works, let's imagine the calculation
for someone whose average indexed monthly earnings were
exactly $6000. The calculation would look like this:

■ 90% of $856 equals $770.40, rounded to $770
■ 32% of $4300 (5157 — 857) equals $1376
■ 15% of $842 (6000 — $5158) equals $126.30,
rounded to $126

That means that this worker's PIA would equal:

$770 + $1376 + $126, for a total of $2272.

That amount is their total monthly benefit if they were to
wait until full retirement age to begin collecting benefits. The
amount would be less if they opted to retire early, and more
if they decided to keep working until the age of 70.

Now let's look at some potential strategies you could use to
help maximize your benefits as a single person.

Keep Working/Delay Collecting

The first option is to continue working as long as you can.
Even if you have already reached full retirement age, you
have the option to continue working until the age of 70. You
do not have to file for benefits at any fixed time.

As previously discussed, the benefit of waiting is that your
monthly payments will accrue at a rate of approximately 8%
per year. If you have the desire and ability to continue
working, you might end up collecting as much as 124% of

your maximum benefit at FRA if you waited until the age of 70 to begin collecting.

You also have the option of waiting to file and begin collecting if you have another means of meeting your monthly expenses if you choose not to continue working. For example, if you have a pension plan or 401k, you might choose to use that to support yourself and delay filing your Social Security claim until later in life.

File and Suspend

Another option open to single people is to file for Social Security benefits and then suspend payments. This option offers retirees the best of both worlds. [46]

Under normal circumstances, Social Security pays only up to six months of benefits retroactively. In other words, if you waited until a year after you reached FRA to file for benefits, you would only receive six months of retroactive benefits. That means there's no real benefit to waiting an artificially long amount of time.

On the other hand, if you reach the age of 66 or 67 – whatever your FRA is — you can file and ask the SSA to suspend payment of your benefits. What this does is allow you to continue to accrue benefits so that when you do begin to collect, you'll have a higher monthly payment than you would have had if you began collecting as soon as you reached your FRA.

That first point is true whether you file and suspend or simply wait to file, but there is another point that can change everything — particularly if you end up encountering unexpected expenses.

People who file and suspend at FRA are eligible to receive FULL back payments at any time in the form of a lump sum payment. The six-month limit on back payments does not apply because the filing happened without delay.

Let's look at an example to understand why this might be helpful. Imagine that Jane reached the age of 66 and decided to file and suspend. She has a modest 401k that allows her to meet her monthly expenses. Her payment at FRA would have been $1800 per month.

Two years later, when she is 68, Jane discovers that she is seriously ill and may not survive much longer. She needs extra money to pay for home health care and other expenses. At that point, she could contact the SSA and request a lump sum payment. For the purposes of this calculation, let's keep it simple and assume a flat payment of $1800 per month. (In a real-life situation, Jane's payments would have been adjusted for inflation and the delay in collection and would be higher in the second year.)

How much would Jane receive? She would get a lump sum payment for 24 full months of benefits, or:

$1800 x 24 months = $43,200

The benefit to Jane is clear. This strategy provides her with a safety net that she can use at any time if she needs it. If she continues to be in good health, she can collect that payment at the age of 70 or simply receive her higher monthly benefits at that point. She won't have to worry about being bankrupted by unexpected expenses because she'll have activated her Social Security benefits as soon as she reached FRA.

This strategy would most likely not work for somebody who was not in a position to work past the age of 62 or who had no source of income other than Social Security. But for someone in Jane's situation, the advantages are undeniable.

Pushing the Reset Button

What if you decided to file for Social Security benefits at the age of 62 and then realized that you had better options available to you? If it has been less than 12 months since you filed, you can file Form 521 with the Social Security Administration and effectively hit the reset button on your benefits. [47]

The way it works is that you will file the form and then repay all of the money you have collected to the Social Security Administration. You have to repay only the amount you received — there is no interest or penalty. You do, however, have to make the payment in a lump sum.

Once you reset your benefits and repay the SSA, you can wait and then file at a later date — when you reach FRA, for example. You may only reset your Social Security benefits once, but it may be helpful if you discover that you are able to support yourself or continue working a bit longer.

Let's look at a couple of examples of situations where hitting the reset button might make sense.

1. Tom just turned 63. He gets laid off from the company where he has worked for 30 years and assumes that he will not be able to find another job because of his age and salary requirements. He decides to file for Social Security benefits. He collects a payment of $2000 per month for five months for a total of $10,000. Then, unexpectedly, he gets a call from a former colleague who offers him a job. The salary is comparable to what he was making before he retired. He could file form 521 and send it to the SSA with a check for $10,000 and then re-file his Social Security claim at a later date.

2. Charlotte has a job she dislikes and she lives modestly. She decides to file for Social Security at the age of 62 so she can stop working. She finds it difficult to get by on her monthly benefit payment. Nine months after she begins collecting, her brother dies and leaves her a nice inheritance. She no longer needs her monthly benefit because she can use her inheritance to support herself. She makes the decision to use part of her inheritance to repay her benefits and delay collecting until she reaches FRA.

Here again, this particular strategy does not apply to people for whom Social Security represents their only form of income. However, for people who regret filing early or unexpectedly discover they have another way to support themselves, hitting the reset button might make sense.

Voluntary Suspension

What happens if you filed for Social Security between the ages of 62 and FRA but it has been more than 12 months since you filed? Hitting the reset button isn't an option, but there is another thing you can do to maximize your benefits. It's called a voluntary suspension. [48]

The way it works is that you can contact the Social Security Administration and suspend the payments you are receiving until you reach FRA. The suspension allows your benefits to continue to accrue, and when you resume them at FRA you will receive a higher monthly payment than you were receiving before the suspension.

Here again, this option might apply if you filed early and then discovered that you were able to support yourself using other means, whether you got a job, inherited money, or even found a way to reduce your monthly living expenses to the point where you could support yourself without Social Security.

Each of these options has its benefits and uses. You should look at all of your options and then make the decision that results in you getting the highest possible benefit while still being able to meet your monthly expenses. It may be that you are not in a position to delay or reset, in which case you should file as soon as possible. If your circumstances change down the line, you can always suspend payments.

Strategies for Married Couples

The strategies for maximizing Social Security change if you are married. Just as there are benefits to filing taxes jointly, there are benefits that you can take advantage of when you file for Social Security.

One thing to keep in mind is that there are family limitations on the amount of Social Security that you can collect under one person's name. We will talk about those in detail in this section so you can take that information into account when you file.

Your goal is always going to be to strike a balance between maximizing your benefits and meeting your expenses, but when you are married you may also want to consider maximizing your spouse's survivor's benefit in the event that you predecease them.

With that in mind, let's look at some strategies for married couples.

Restricted Application

This first strategy is available to you only if you reached the age of 62 prior to January 2, 2016. [49] This strategy works best if one spouse's benefits are significantly higher than the other's.

Let's imagine a married couple, Bill and Amy. Bill has earned close to the maximum taxable amount for most of his working life, while Amy's income has been significantly lower. Bill wants to do whatever he can to maximize the survivor benefit Amy will collect if she outlives him.

Once Amy reaches Full Retirement Age, she files for benefits. Bill, provided he is at least 66 years old, can file a restricted application that allows him to collect only spousal benefits. If Amy's payment is $1800 per month, Bill would be eligible to receive 50% of Amy's PIA, or $900. That would put their combined benefits, as a couple, at $2700 per month.

If this combined income allows them to pay their monthly expenses, Bill may continue to let his benefits accrue until he reaches the age of 70, at which point he would file to receive his own benefits and no longer be eligible for spousal benefits. His monthly payment is $3000.

At that point, Amy would continue to receive her monthly benefit of $1800, and Bill would receive his full monthly benefit of $3000, increasing their total income to $4800. This switch would also mean that if Bill dies before Amy does, she could collect a survivor's benefit of $2250, significantly more than her solo benefit of $1800.

It is important to note that this strategy works best if one spouse's benefit is higher than the other's, but not so much higher that the lower-earning spouse would be better off with a spousal benefit. In other words, if Amy's monthly benefit were less than half of Bill's, she would be better off filing for spousal benefits than she would be collecting her own worker's benefit.

Again, please note that this strategy does not apply to you if you have not reached the age of 62 prior to January 2, 2016. The same rule changes that eliminated the file and suspend option, which allowed the higher-earning spouse to file for benefits, suspend payments to continue to accrue benefits, and still allow their spouse to collect spousal benefits also changed this rule. People who met the age requirement at the time of the rule change were grandfathered in, but this option does not apply to anybody who was younger than 62 on January 2, 2016.

Delay to Increase Lifetime Benefits
If both spouses are in good health and still able to work, then there is a significant benefit to delaying the collection of benefits as long as possible. Imagine a couple, Lucy and Edward, who have respective monthly benefits at FRA of $2200 and $2000. They are both 66 years old, with birthdays just a month apart from one another.

They look at their finances and decide that they want to keep working until they are 70 years old. At that point, Lucy's benefits will have grown to $2728 and Edward's will have grown to $2480.

Assuming that each of them lives until the age of 90, they would have increased their benefits dramatically. If they collected at the age of 66, they would collectively receive 24 years of benefits at a combined rate of $4200 per month for a total of $1,209,600.

If they delay collecting until they are both 70, they would receive 20 years of benefits at the increased rate of $5208 per month. That would put their total lifetime benefits at $1,249,920. Collectively, they would receive a little more than $40,000 in additional benefits over that time.

For couples in good health who have decent life expectancies, this strategy is a good way to ensure that you have the biggest possible payout to cover your living expenses even if you both live to a ripe old age. It also has the benefit of maximizing survivor benefits for both parties, so regardless of which partner predeceases the other, the survivor will be able to collect a substantial benefit after their partner dies.

Claim Early Due to Health Concerns
If one or both partners are in poor or failing health, then the best strategy might be to claim as soon as possible after they turn 62 to maximize payments during their lifetimes. This is a tricky call because the payments do increase dramatically after you reach full retirement age. But when one partner, or both partners, has a shortened life expectancy due to illness, there is no real benefit to delaying the collection of benefits.

For example, say that Charlie and Rose both have health issues. Charlie has congestive heart failure. He takes medication and manages his diet, but his life expectancy is not particularly long. Rose has diabetes and rheumatoid arthritis. If they were to delay collecting their benefits, they might collect far less if they die early than they would if they began collecting early.

Even if they have other means of supporting themselves, there are benefits to filing and collecting benefits as soon as possible. The additional money they receive each month may help them to cover medical expenses and other needs, and thus maximize their quality of life as long as they are alive.

Maximize Survivor Benefits
The importance of survivor benefits increases when the gap between two spouses' PIAs increases. If you are married and your benefits are significantly higher than your spouse's, then it may make sense to delay filing as long as you can in order to maximize the survivor's benefit, particularly if you have dependent children.

In some cases, the decision may be obvious. If Steven and Jessica are married and Jessica stopped working when she was 30 because they decided that she would be a stay-at-home mother to their children, Steven's Social Security benefit is likely to be much higher than Jessica's.

In such a case, Steven would likely to want to delay collecting benefits as long as possible in order to maximize Jessica's survivor's benefit.

The urgency might be just as high if Steven and Jessica had an adult child who was disabled or if they were financially responsible for one or more aging parents. The higher Steven's monthly payout is, the more money there will be available for his family.

Keep Family Maximums in Mind

The maximum benefit payable to a single family is calculated in a way that is similar to the PIA calculation. [50]

The primary difference is that there are three bend points instead of two. The three bend points as of 2016 were:

- 150% of the first $1093
- 272% of the difference between $1094 and the second bend point of $1578
- 134% of the difference between $1579 and the third bend point of $2058
- 175% of any amount over $2058

The following chart illustrates the bend points:

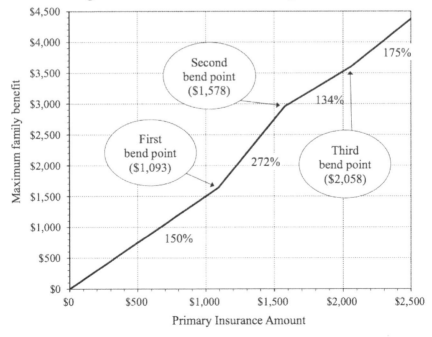

Let's look at an example, since it might be difficult to understand how it would work. Imagine that Steven's PIA is $3000 per month if he waits to collect until he turns 70. All items are rounded to the nearest ten cents. That would break down as follows:

- 150% of the first $1093 equals $1639.50

- 272% of the next $484 (the difference between the first and second bend points) equals $1316.48, which is rounded to $1316.50

- 134% of the next $479 (the difference between the second and third bend points) equals $641.86, which is rounded to $641.90

- 175% of the next $941 (the difference between the third bend point and Steven's PIA) equals $1646.75 which is rounded to $1,646.80

That means that the maximum monthly benefit for Steven's entire family, including Jessica and their children, would be:

$1639.50 + $1316.30 + 641.90 + $1646.80, for a total of $5,244.50.

Keep in mind that Jessica is eligible to receive 50% of Steven's PIA as a spousal benefit while he is alive, and 82.5% after he is dead, provided she is over her FRA and not remarried. Each of their children, if they are eligible, might receive up to 75% of Steven's PIA as a benefit. However, the entire family, combined, may not receive more than $5,244.50.

If Steven were to predecease Jessica, she would receive $2475 in survivor's benefits. If they had three children under the age of 18 who were all full-time students, each child would be eligible to receive $2250. However, the combined total in that case would exceed the family maximum:

$2475 + $2250 + 2250 + $2250 = $9,225.

This benefit would be reduced proportionally. Jessica's payment would remain the same, but the payment released to each child would be reduced proportionally. Since Jessica's benefit is $2475, that leaves a total of $2769.50 to be split among their three children. Each child would get one-third of that amount until they turned 18 and were no longer eligible, as follows:

$2769.50 / 3 = $923.17

The benefit received would be adjusted as each child reached maturity. So when their oldest child turned 19 or left school (whichever came first) the total family benefit (less Jessica's benefit) would be divided between the two remaining children.

It is important to note here that if either spouse has an ex-spouse who files a spousal claim, the amount paid to them does not count toward the family total. That person, while eligible, is not considered to be part of the family unit.

Any family with dependent children, dependent parents, or dependent grandchildren should take the maximum family benefit into consideration when planning for retirement.

Strategies for Divorced People and Widows/Widowers
The final category to consider when it comes to strategy is for people who are either divorced or have been widowed. There are a few special considerations, although many of the practical considerations may still apply.

How to Determine if Filing for Spousal Benefits Helps You
We already talked about eligibility for spousal benefits after divorce. As a reminder, you must have been married for 10 or more years, and you must be 62 years old or older. In the event that your ex-spouse has not yet filed for benefits, you may still file if you have been divorced for at least two years.

It benefits you to file for spousal benefits if the amount you would be eligible to collect under your spousal benefit exceeds what you would be eligible to receive based on your own work history. The payment for spousal benefits for divorced people is the same as it is for married people: 50% of their PIA.

If Melissa is divorced from Harry, she should look at her own PIA and his and determine which option will result in the highest monthly payout for her. If Harry's PIA is $2800, her payout would be $1400. Her own PIA might be only $1200, in which case it makes perfect sense for her to file for spousal benefits.

Note that Melissa will receive 50% of Harry's PIA if she waits until full retirement age to collect. If she files early, the amount she collects will be reduced by approximately 8% per year.

The payouts work by delivering first the amount of the worker's benefits, and then making up the difference from the ex-spouse's benefits. So in our example, Melissa would receive $1200 of her benefit first, and then an additional $200 per month from Harry's Social Security.

It is important to note here that it doesn't matter if Harry has more than one ex-wife. Both women may file for spousal benefits. There is no need to inform Harry that they are doing so, nor can he do anything to deny their eligibility. Remember, the benefits Melissa collects will not change Harry's benefits, or the benefits that his new wife or children may collect.

Collecting for Dependent Children

If you are divorced or widowed and have the responsibility of caring for any of your spouse's dependent children under the age of 16, you may collect benefits to help you support them. Additionally, surviving children under the age of 18 may collect, as previously discussed, a maximum of 75% of the deceased parent's PIA — subject to change based on the family maximum.

This is a fairly simple calculation and there is no good argument for not filing for this benefit if you have children under the age of 16. The extra money you receive may help

offset the expenses associated with raising a child and —
again — these benefits will not reduce or in any way alter
the amount that your spouse's current family can receive.

File and Delay

In the event that you were born before January 2, 1954, you
have the option of filing to collect spousal benefits and
delaying your own benefits until you reach FRA.
However, anybody born after that date does not have this
option. You must file for a spousal benefit if you are eligible
to collect more than you would under your own worker's
benefit. If not, you will be eligible only for your own benefit.

If you have remarried, then you are not eligible to collect
spousal benefits. However, if your remarriage ends in death
or divorce, then you may still be able to collect spousal
benefits — even if you have previously become ineligible
due to remarriage. [51]

If you want to file for spousal benefits, you will need to
provide the SSA with:

- Your birth certificate
- Your marriage certificate
- Your divorce decree
- Your ex-spouse's Social Security number

If you do not have your ex-spouse's SSN, you may be asked
for other qualifying information such as their full name,
birth date, and parents' names so that the SSA can look them
up.

The notes here about ex-spouses may also apply in the event that your ex-spouse dies, particularly if there is a financial relationship between you. If you were dependent upon your ex for alimony, you may be eligible for benefits.

The next chapter will look at another important topic when it comes to maximizing your benefits. While you will have to pay some taxes, there are things you can do to minimize your tax payments — and I'll tell you what you need to know to accomplish that.

Still Confused About Benefits?

Our website can give you another review of how benefits work with interactive charts, calculators, and planning tools. You can even connect with a Consultant to get a free benefits report!

Visit www.SocialSecuritySupport.com

Chapter 7
Social Security Tax Reduction Strategies

When it comes to maximizing your Social Security benefits, you need to give some consideration to taxes. Taxes are a major concern for anybody who is contemplating retirement. While we all have to pay our fair share, the truth is that many of us end up paying more than we need to simply because we don't understand the rules.

This chapter will look at some of the strategies you can use to reduce your Social Security taxes and thus maximize your benefits.

Combined Income Formula

The first thing you need to know is that you may have to pay some taxes on your Social Security benefits if you have other forms of income that you have to report to the IRS. [52]

Those forms of income may include:

- Wages
- Self-employment
- Interest
- Dividends
- Any other form of income that is taxable

However, nobody has to pay taxes on more than 85% of their Social Security benefit. The formula you can use to calculate it is as follows:

Adjusted Gross Income	+	Nontaxable Interest	+	½ of your Social Security benefits	=	Combined Income

As you can see, your combined income equals:

- Your adjusted gross income +
- Non-taxable interest +
- ½ of your Social Security benefits

The way this rule works is that if you are single and your combined income is between $25,000 and $34,000, you may have to pay taxes on up to 50% of your Social Security benefits. If your combined income is more than $34,000, you may have to pay taxes on up to 85% of your Social Security benefits.

If you are married and file a joint return, you and your spouse may have to pay taxes as well. The limits are higher for married couples. If your combined income is between $32,000 and $44,000, you may have to pay taxes on up to 50% of your Social Security benefits; and if your combined income is over $44,000, you may have to pay taxes on up to 85% of your Social Security benefits.

If you do not have any other forms of income, then it is likely that you will not have to pay taxes on your Social Security benefits.

How IRA and 401k Withdrawals Affect Social Security Taxes

If you have an Individual Retirement Account (IRA) or 401k account, then withdrawals you make from those accounts may affect the taxes you have to pay on your Social Security benefits. [53]

Withdrawing money from traditional retirement accounts, whether you have a 401k, a traditional IRA, or some other kind of account, will not in any way reduce the amount of the benefits you are eligible to receive. However, if you take large withdrawals in one year that lead to a combined income that exceeds the amounts laid out in the previous section, you will have to pay taxes on those withdrawals.

For example, if you were collecting Social Security benefits of $2000 per month and you also withdrew $20,000 from an IRA, your combined income would be:

$20,000 (your adjusted gross income) + $12,000 (50% of your total Social Security benefits for the year) = $32,000

For the sake of simplifying the formula, I have assumed that there was no non-taxable interest to add to the formula. Based on the rules for combined income, you might have to pay taxes on up to 50% of your Social Security benefits because your combined income falls between $25,000 and $34,000.

The one exception here is the Roth IRA, which has no impact on your taxable income. You can withdraw as much as you like from a Roth IRA and it will not reduce your benefits or increase your tax burden.

The best thing to do if you have additional retirement funds is to space out withdrawals if you can. If you can keep your withdrawals to a level where your combined income is below the thresholds mentioned here, then you can avoid paying taxes on your Social Security benefits.

I also want to make a note here that certain kinds of retirement plans can actually reduce the amount of benefits you are eligible to receive. For example, if you worked for the government and received a pension that was not subject to Social Security taxes, your PIA would be reduced by two-thirds of the amount of the pension. The same might apply if you worked for a foreign employer. It's called the Government Pension Offset (GPO). [54] Let's look at an example:

You are eligible for Social Security benefits of $1500, and you also receive a government pension that totals $1200. Your Social Security benefit would be reduced by two-thirds of the pension, or $800, but you would still receive the full amount of the pension. In other words, your total monthly payment would be:

($1500 — $800) + $1200, or a total of $1900

The result is that you still get a higher income than you would on Social Security alone, but the SSA withholds something to account for the fact that you did not pay Social Security taxes on the pension amount.

Examples of Tax Reduction

The following graphs demonstrate how two different retirement strategies can have a massive impact on your tax liability.

Example A

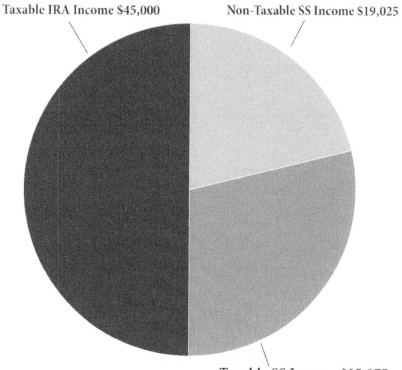

Taxable IRA Income $45,000   Non-Taxable SS Income $19,025

Taxable SS Income $25,975

In Example A the taxable income is **$70,975** with a total tax bill of **$10,772**. This is due to a high reliance on taxable IRA income.

Example B

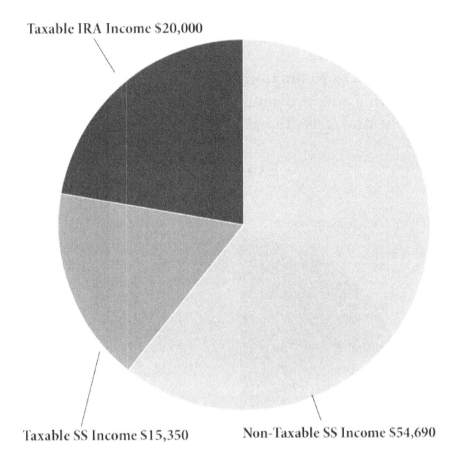

Taxable IRA Income $20,000

Taxable SS Income $15,350

Non-Taxable SS Income $54,690

Example B meanwhile reduces the reliance on IRA income and instead produces a tax liability of **$35,350** with total taxes on income being **$2,392**.

Both plans produce **$90,000** in annual benefits. Only one gives you **$8,830** in extra income a year. Over a 10-year period that's over **$80,000** dollars in extra income!

Continuing to Work While Collecting

In some cases, you may wish to continue working while you receive Social Security benefits. For example, some people who retire after a long career may decide that they want to pursue other work on a part-time or full-time basis.

If you are over full retirement age, then there is no limit on your earnings. However, if you are younger than full retirement age or reach full retirement age in 2020, then some of your benefits may be withheld as follows: [55]

Your Age in 2019	Your Earning Limit
Full retirement age or older	No limit on earnings
Younger than full retirement age	For every $2 over the limit of $17,640, $1 is withheld from benefits until the month you reach full retirement age.
You reach full retirement age in 2019	For every $3 over the limit of $46,920, $1 is withheld from benefits until the month you reach full retirement age.

Let's spell it out to be sure you understand it. In 2019, the limit on earnings outside of Social Security was $17,640. A retiree who was under FRA for the entire year and earned more than that amount would have their benefits reduced by one dollar for every two dollars over that limit he earned.

In other words, if he earned a total of $20,000 working part time, he would be $2,360 over the annual limit. He would therefore experience a reduction in his benefits totaling half of that amount, or $1,180. The reduction would be spaced out over 12 months.

The rules are slightly different if he reached retirement age in 2019. In that case, he would have a higher limit of $41,920 on his earnings, and that total would apply only to the months he worked before he reached FRA. If he earned more than that amount, he would receive a reduction in benefits of one dollar for every three dollars over that he earned.

These reductions apply only before you reach FRA. After FRA, there is no limit to the amount of income you may earn, and no reduction in benefits — as is demonstrated by this chart.

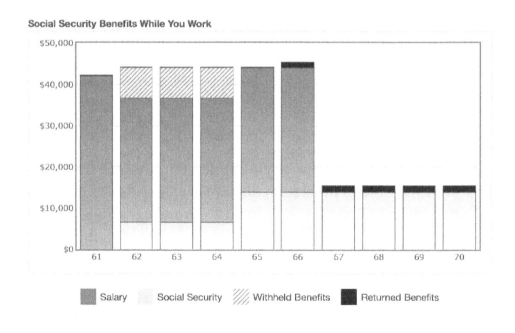

I also want to note that there is some benefit to continuing to work, as you will continue to pay Social Security taxes (as will your employer) on your income. If you work enough, the additional income you earn may lead to an increase in your monthly benefit. That can be a significant help to people who have had some low income years, since you may recall that Social Security benefits are based on your average income for your 35 highest-earning years.

The primary concern here is to do what you can to avoid paying taxes on your Social Security benefits. If you have time before retirement, you may want to consider opening a Roth IRA so that you can withdraw money as needed without having to pay taxes on your benefits.

Alternatively, it may help to work out as much of a retirement plan as you can so that you can space out your withdrawals from traditional IRAs or 401k accounts to keep your combined income under the limit.

It may help to consult with a professional retirement planner on these points to determine the best way to minimize your tax burden. It is never going to be possible to predict exactly what you will need in terms of withdrawals from other retirement accounts as unforeseeable circumstances may affect your decisions. However, if you do some preliminary planning and strategizing now, you are less likely to get hit with a huge tax bill as the result of a withdrawal.

Need Help with Your Tax Planning?

Our website features a variety of tools to help you plan for taxes. You can also get connected with a Certified Advisor who could provide you an even more complete overview of your tax options.

Visit www.SocialSecuritySupport.com

Bonus Chapter
What Happens Next

The information contained in this book may be a bit overwhelming. I think you can see why my friend was so confused and scared when she started to think about Social Security — and why I was so eager to help her figure it out. Even for me, navigating the thousands of Social Security rules and regulations was a daunting task, and I do this for a living. It's no wonder that the average person is intimidated by the process.

In this final chapter, I'm going to share some general resources and information to help answer your questions and provide you with some guidance to get you through the process of making decisions about Social Security and filing for benefits.

Getting a Statement of Benefits
The Social Security Administration mails regular statements of benefits to everyone with a Social Security Number. As a rule, the statements are mailed every five years, so you should receive one about three months prior to your birthday when you turn 25, 30, 35, and so on.

If you have not received a statement or simply want an updated one, there are several ways to do it.

1. Go to the SSA website. Sign up for an account and request a statement.
2. If you prefer not to request a statement online, you can print out a form from their website, fill it out and mail it in to request a statement. It will take about four to six weeks to arrive.
3. Your third option is to go to a financial advisor, preferably one with a Social Security certification, and have them request a statement for you.

It is definitely a good idea to get the most recent statement possible as you can use the information on it to determine the most likely amount of your benefits and start making strategic decisions about the best retirement option for you, your spouse, and your family.

BONUS

Visit www.SocialSecuritySupport.com

Get tips on reducing and how to avoid paying unnecessary taxes on your Social Security!

Discover:

- How to avoid unnecessary taxes
- How to increase your benefits by up to $100,00
- How to avoid Social Security penalties
- The 500 options for taking Social Security
- How working will affect your benefits
- The latest changes to Social Security Law

Have a Certified Social Security Expert Provide You a Customized Social Security Report!

Get a Free Personalized Report
Sign Up BELOW to connect with a NSSA CERTIFIED ADVISOR

SEND MY FREE REPORT

Certified Advisor

Sign Up and Get Connected!

Frequently Asked Questions

Now let's run through a few of the most commonly asked questions about Social Security. I have addressed some of them already, but I think it's helpful to have them all together in one place.

When Should I File for Social Security?

This is by far the most common question I get as an adviser, and as you know from reading the book there is no one-size-fits-all answer. However, a good rule of thumb is that if you are willing and able to continue working, your best bet is probably to keep working at least until you reach full retirement age, and beyond if you can. The longer you work, the higher your monthly benefit will be.

People who are unable to work or are ill may be better off filing as soon as they reach the age of 62. Remember, you have the option of undoing your filing and reimbursing the SSA within one year if your situation changes.

How Much Will I Receive from Social Security?

The next question is almost as common as the first, and depends greatly upon the number of years you have worked and how much you earned in that time. As I mentioned previously, your Social Security benefit will be based upon your average income in the 35 years when you earned the most money after adjustment for inflation. The longer you work, the higher your benefit will be.

The amount you receive if you retire early and begin collecting at the age of 62 may be significantly lower than it would be if you waited until full retirement age — and even lower when compared to what your monthly benefit would be if you waited until you were 70 years old to begin collecting.

Depending upon your marital status and your spouse's benefits, you may end up being better off filing for spousal benefits than relying on your own Social Security. However, remember that if you have your own benefit you will always collect it first, and then receive a monthly supplement from your spouse's benefits to bring you up to the maximum allowable to you as a spouse.

Can I Still Work While Collecting Social Security?

As mentioned in the previous chapter, you may still work while collecting Social Security benefits. However, there is a limit on the amount you may earn if you are under full retirement age, and you may have to pay taxes on a portion of your benefits. At most, you may be taxed on 85% of your benefits.

It is also important to note that after you reach full retirement age, the Social Security Administration will stop taxing you on additional income and will also increase your monthly benefits to pay you back for the amount of benefits that were withheld as a result of you working.

Can I Collect Spousal Benefits If I'm Divorced?

Can I Collect Spousal Benefits If I'm Divorced?

You may collect spousal benefits if you are divorced if you are over the age of 62, you were married for at least 10 years, and you have been divorced for at least two years. (If you have not been divorced for two years, you may still file once you reach full retirement age.) You may not have remarried. Any benefits you collect as a divorced spouse will not accrue toward the maximum family limit for your ex-spouse's new spouse or dependent children.

Can I Collect Social Security if I Have Never Worked?

If you are married but have never worked, you qualify to collect a spousal benefit equivalent to 50% of your spouse's benefit. You will be subject to reductions in your benefit if you file before you reach full retirement age. However, if you wait until full retirement age, you may collect the full 50% of your spouse's PIA.

What Happens if My Spouse Dies Before Retirement?

Losing a spouse can be traumatic enough without having to worry about money. If your spouse dies before reaching full retirement age, you may still qualify for a spousal benefit as a survivor, provided you have not remarried by the time you are eligible to file.

The amount that you can collect depends upon how old you are when you file and whether you have dependent children under the age of 16 at the time of your spouse's death. If you are at full retirement age you can collect 100% of your spouse's PIA. If you are between the age of 60 and FRA, you can collect 71.5% of their benefit, and if you have dependent children you may collect 75% of their PIA, regardless of your age.

Can I Have Federal Income Tax Withheld from My Payments?

If you know that you will be exceeding the annual income limits due to IRA withdrawals or some other form of income, you may choose to have federal taxes withheld from your Social Security payments to offset the amount you owe. If you choose to do this, you'll need to download a form from the IRS and send it to the SSA.

You may have other questions, and if you do you can find answers by visiting this books website which is located at www.SocialSecuritySupport.com

Definitions

To close out the book, I also want to give you some definitions in glossary form so that you can refer to it as needed. At the end of this section, I'll give you a link to a full glossary of terms on the Social Security Administration's website.

Full Retirement Age or FRA

Full Retirement Age is the age at which you become eligible to collect 100% of your benefits without reduction. As a reminder, here is the chart showing Full Retirement Age based on your birth year. People who were born after 1960 will not reach FRA until their 67th birthdays.

Year of Birth	Full Retirement Age
1943-1954	66
1955	66 & 2 Months
1956	66 & 4 Months
1957	66 & 6 Months
1958	66 & 8 Months
1959	66 & 10 Months
1960 or Later	67

Primary Insurance Amount or PIA

The Primary Insurance Amount is the amount of your Social Security benefit if you chose to begin collecting as soon as you reached your FRA. This amount is not reduced as a result of early collection nor augmented as a result of delaying collection.

In addition to being used as the basis of your benefits, your PIA is also used to calculate spousal, dependent, and survivor benefits.

Combined Income Formula or CIF

The Combined Income Formula is the formula used to determine if you must pay taxes on some portion of your Social Security benefits. If Social Security is your only form of income you will not be taxed. However, if you have other retirement accounts, non-taxable interest, or if you continue working, you may be taxed on up to 85% of your Social Security benefits.

Cost of Living Adjustment or COLA

The Cost of Living Adjustment is the adjustment to your PIA based on cost of living increases. However, as of 2016 these adjustments are linked to the Consumer Price Index and are likely to be significantly smaller than they were in the past.

Consumer Price Index or CPI

The Consumer Price Index is a measure of the average cost of consumer goods and has historically been used to calculate the COLA for Social Security recipients. However, as of 2016 the SSA is using a chained CPI, which assumes that retirees will make other adjustments to account for inflation — such as buying less-expensive versions of products.

Sources

1. Social Security. (n.d.). Retrieved January 09, 2017, from https://www.ssa.gov/history/briefhistory3.html
2. English Poor Laws. (2016, December 01). Retrieved January 09, 2017, from http://socialwelfare.library.vcu.edu/programs/poor-laws/
3. Social Security. (n.d.). Retrieved January 09, 2017, from https://www.ssa.gov/history/tpaine3.html
4. Social Security. (n.d.). Retrieved January 09, 2017, from https://www.ssa.gov/history/puck.html
5. Social Security. (n.d.). Retrieved January 09, 2017, from https://www.ssa.gov/history/briefhistory3.html
6. Social Security. (n.d.). Retrieved January 09, 2017, from https://www.ssa.gov/history/briefhistory3.html
7. Social Security. (n.d.). Retrieved January 09, 2017, from https://www.ssa.gov/history/briefhistory3.html
8. Social Security. (n.d.). Retrieved January 09, 2017, from https://www.ssa.gov/history/briefhistory3.html
9. Social Security. (n.d.). Retrieved January 09, 2017, from https://www.ssa.gov/history/briefhistory3.html
10. Social Security. (n.d.). Retrieved January 09, 2017, from https://www.ssa.gov/history/fdrsignstate.html
11. Social Security. (n.d.). Retrieved January 09, 2017, from https://www.ssa.gov/history/briefhistory3.html
12. Social Security. (n.d.). Retrieved January 09, 2017, from https://www.ssa.gov/history/briefhistory3.html
13. Social Security. (n.d.). Retrieved January 09, 2017, from https://www.ssa.gov/history/briefhistory3.html
14. Social Security. (n.d.). Retrieved January 09, 2017, from https://www.ssa.gov/history/briefhistory3.html

15. Social Security Administration. (n.d.). Retrieved January 09, 2017, from https://www.ssa.gov/policy/docs/chartbooks/fast_facts/2016/fast_facts16.html#contributions

16. Caplinger, D. (2014, August 25). Need Social Security Advice? Don't Just Go to the Obvious Source. Retrieved January 09, 2017, from http://www.fool.com/retirement/general/2014/08/25/need-social-security-advice-dont-just-go-to-the-ob.aspx

17. Zhang, H. (2016, July 28). Low interest rates a growing threat to Social Security. Retrieved January 09, 2017, from http://www.marketwatch.com/story/low-interest-rates-a-growing-threat-to-social-security-2016-07-28

18. A. (2016, November 17). Fighting to Keep Medicare and Social Security Strong. Retrieved January 09, 2017, from http://www.aarp.org/politics-society/advocacy/info-2016/where-aarp-stands-on-medicare-social-security.html

19. Campbell, T. (2016, January 31). How Big Is the Average Social Security Check? Retrieved January 09, 2017, from http://www.fool.com/investing/general/2016/01/31/how-big-is-the-average-social-security-check.aspx

20. H. (n.d.). Make Sure The Retirement Crisis Doesn't Happen to You. Retrieved January 09, 2017, from https://www.thebalance.com/retirement-crisis-stats-causes-effect-3306215

21. 2017 Social Security Changes. (n.d.). Retrieved January 09, 2017, from

https://www.ssa.gov/news/press/factsheets/colafacts2017.pdf

22. http://www.fool.com/retirement/2016/12/04/what-is-your-social-security-retirement-age.aspx

23. Kotlikoff, L. J., Moeller, P., & Solman, P. (2015). *Get What's Yours: The Secrets to Maxing Out Your Social Security*. Simon and Schuster.

24. Kotlikoff, L. J., Moeller, P., & Solman, P. (2015). *Get What's Yours: The Secrets to Maxing Out Your Social Security*. Simon and Schuster.

25. Social Security. (n.d.). Retrieved January 09, 2017, from https://www.ssa.gov/oact/cola/colaseries.html

26. Kotlikoff, L. J., Moeller, P., & Solman, P. (2015). *Get What's Yours: The Secrets to Maxing Out Your Social Security*. Simon and Schuster.

27. Kotlikoff, L. J., Moeller, P., & Solman, P. (2015). *Get What's Yours: The Secrets to Maxing Out Your Social Security*. Simon and Schuster.

28. Landis, A. (2016). *Social Security: The Inside Story.* MBI Publishing Company.

29. News and Research Communications. (n.d.). Retrieved January 09, 2017, from http://oregonstate.edu/ua/ncs/archives/2016/apr/working-longer-may-lead-longer-life-new-osu-research-shows

30. Life Expectancy. (2016, October 07). Retrieved January 09, 2017, from https://www.cdc.gov/nchs/fastats/life-expectancy.htm

31. Sample Social Security Statement of Benefits. (n.d.). Retrieved January 09, 2017, from https://www.ssa.gov/myaccount/materials/pdfs/SSA-

7005-SM-
SI%20Wanda%20Worker%20Near%20retirement.pdf

32. Social Security. (n.d.). Retrieved January 09, 2017, from https://www.ssa.gov

33. Landis, A. (2016). *Social Security: The Inside Story.* MBI Publishing Company.

34. Landis, A. (2016). *Social Security: The Inside Story.* MBI Publishing Company.

35. What Same Sex Couples Need to Know. (n.d.). Retrieved January 09, 2017, from https://www.ssa.gov/pubs/EN-05-10014.pdf

36. Social Security. (n.d.). Retrieved January 09, 2017, from https://www.ssa.gov/planners/retire/yourdivspouse.html

37. Social Security. (n.d.). Retrieved January 09, 2017, from https://www.ssa.gov/planners/retire/yourchildren.html

38. Landis, A. (2016). *Social Security: The Inside Story.* MBI Publishing Company.

39. Landis, A. (2016). *Social Security: The Inside Story.* MBI Publishing Company.

40. Social Security. (n.d.). Retrieved January 09, 2017, from https://www.ssa.gov/planners/survivors/onyourown2.html

41. Social Security. (n.d.). Retrieved January 09, 2017, from https://www.ssa.gov/planners/survivors/onyourown3.html

42. Social Security. (n.d.). Retrieved January 09, 2017, from https://www.ssa.gov/planners/survivors/onyourown4.html

43. Social Security. (n.d.). Retrieved January 09, 2017, from https://faq.ssa.gov/link/portal/34011/34019/Article/3766/Who-can-get-Social-Security-survivors-benefits-and-how-do-I-apply

44. Landis, A. (2016). *Social Security: The Inside Story.* MBI Publishing Company.

45. Social Security. (n.d.). Retrieved January 09, 2017, from https://www.ssa.gov/OACT/COLA/piaformula.html

46. Social Security. (n.d.). Retrieved January 09, 2017, from https://www.ssa.gov/planners/retire/suspend.html

47. Social Security. (n.d.). Retrieved January 09, 2017, from https://www.ssa.gov/planners/retire/withdrawal.html

48. Social Security. (n.d.). Retrieved January 09, 2017, from https://www.ssa.gov/planners/retire/suspend.html

49. Landis, A. (2016). *Social Security: The Inside Story.* MBI Publishing Company.

50. Landis, A. (2016). *Social Security: The Inside Story.* MBI Publishing Company.

51. Social Security. (n.d.). Retrieved January 09, 2017, from https://www.ssa.gov/survivors/

52. Landis, A. (2016). *Social Security: The Inside Story.* MBI Publishing Company.

53. Staff, M. F. (n.d.). Does an IRA Distribution Count As Income to Social Security? Retrieved January 09, 2017, from http://www.fool.com/knowledge-center/does-an-ira-distribution-count-as-income-to-social.aspx

54. Social Security. (n.d.). Retrieved January 09, 2017, from https://www.ssa.gov/planners/retire/gpo-calc.html

55. How Work Affects Your Benefits. (n.d.). Retrieved January 09, 2017, from https://www.ssa.gov/pubs/EN-05-10069.pdf

Thank you for reading *7 Paths to Maximizing Social Security*. I hope that you have found the information in this book to be helpful.

My goal is to help demystify and simplify the process of figuring out the best way to maximize your Social Security. That said, the information contained here is necessarily incomplete. As I said before, there are thousands of rules and regulations governing the filing and payment of Social Security benefits. It is not possible to cover all of them here.

If there is any topic that you have questions about that I did not cover in my book, you may be able to find it at www.SocialSecuritySupport.com

You may also want to consider calling a Financial Advisor, particularly one that is certified to assist people with Social Security. Remember, employees of the SSA cannot give you advice about the best way to file for your benefits — and even if they do, their advice may not actually be a reflection of what's best for you. If you are uncertain about how to proceed or want additional guidance, seek help from a professional who understands the system and how it works.

Thank you again for reading — to your continued success.

Tony J. Hansmann

Book Tony To Speak!

Book Tony Hansmann as your Keynote Speaker and You're Guaranteed to Make Your Event Memorable!

For the past 16 years Tony Hansmann has provided expert Social Security information nationwide on Television, Print, Radio and seminars.

To have Tony speak contact his booking agent at 479-268-4463.

Made in the USA
Monee, IL
12 May 2020